Creative FOLK ART

by Sue Iliov

A J.B. Fairfax Press Publication

CONTENTS

CONTENTS

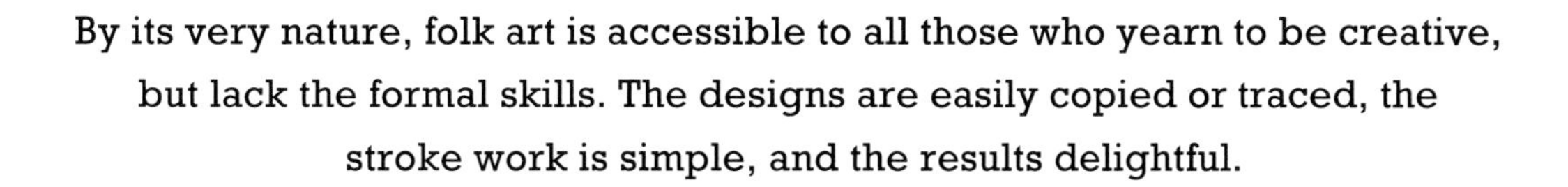

By its very nature, folk art is accessible to all those who yearn to be creative, but lack the formal skills. The designs are easily copied or traced, the stroke work is simple, and the results delightful.

EDITORIAL
Managing Editor: Judy Poulos
Editorial Assistant: Ella Martin
Editorial Coordinator: Margaret Kelly
Photography: Neil Lorimer
Styling: Judy Ostergard
Illustrations: Judy Ostergard

DESIGN AND PRODUCTION
Production Manager: Anna Maguire
Design: Jenny Nossal
Cover Design: Jenny Pace

Production Editor: Sheridan Packer
Design Manager: Drew Buckmaster
Production Coordinator: Sophie Potter

Published by J.B. Fairfax Press Pty Limited
80-82 McLachlan Ave
Rushcutters Bay NSW 2011, Australia
A.C.N. 003 738 430
Formatted by J.B. Fairfax Press Pty Limited

Printed by Toppan Printing Company, Singapore

JBFP 474

CREATIVE FOLK ART
ISBN 1 86343 301 5

DISTRIBUTION AND SALES
Ph: (02) 9361 6366 Fax: (02) 9360 6262
Web: http://www.jbfp.com.au

INTRODUCTION

I discovered folk art seven years ago when I passed a sign in my local craft shop which claimed that I could learn to paint in four lessons. I enrolled in the classes and, after only one lesson, I was addicted. In my first four lessons, I learnt the basic brush strokes and painted my first project. Of course, it takes more than four lessons to learn to paint – there is always so much more to learn – but this first beginner's class gave me a taste of the huge scope that folk art encompasses.

There are so many different traditional and regional styles and so many decorative artists producing innovative work of their own that I find it impossible to define any one style that appeals to me above all the others. In this book, therefore, I have painted projects using a wide variety of styles of folk art, but almost all have a rich, aged or antique appearance, either in the colours used or in the finishing processes.

The projects range from those which are suitable for confident beginners through to more difficult pieces. I encourage you to be creative with the projects and patterns. Experiment with using different colourings and adapting the designs to suit your own taste. Paint to please yourself!

Sue

TERMS AND TECHNIQUES

I want to subtitle this section 'When all else fails, read the instructions'. If you are like me, you probably don't want to waste precious painting time reading pages of instructions, but would rather get out your palette and brushes and launch straight into it. However, please take a little time to read the following notes on the terms and techniques, especially if you are fairly new to folk art.

EQUIPMENT

BRUSHES

Most of the projects in this book are painted using round brush techniques; flat brushes are used only occasionally for a little shading. I use a round Raphael Kolinsky brush, Series 8404 size 3, for all my round-brush work and a synthetic liner brush, also Raphael, Series 8224 size 0, for fine painting. The Raphael Kolinsky is a sable brush with a fine tip and longer bristles than many round brushes (especially synthetic ones), which makes it very versatile. I can paint fine lacework using this brush, as well as wide comma strokes. If you prefer to use a synthetic brush, you will need a size 4 brush for the projects in this book.

Other brushes you will need are:

- Synthetic flat brushes sizes 6 and 8, which are used mostly for floating colour for shading and highlighting.
- A range of bristle brushes (hogs hair) up to 2.5 cm (1 in), either round or flat, are extremely versatile. They are inexpensive brushes, so it is well worth buying a range of different sizes and shapes. I often use them for base-painting projects, especially when I want to create a textured background. They are ideal for dry-brushing techniques as well.
- Filbert brushes sizes 4 and 6 are similar to flat brushes except that the tip of the bristles is rounded rather than square. They help give a rounded beginning to your brush strokes. This is very useful, especially for painting the Zhostova floral style on the chocolate box project on page 19.
- A 2.5 cm (1 in) synthetic flat brush is useful for varnishing.

I like to use Jo Sonja's paints and mediums and all the projects in the book are painted with these. I especially like using Jo Sonja's Flow Medium and Jo Sonja's Clear Glazing Medium. Adding flow medium to your paints makes them glide onto your painting surface without becoming transparent (which happens when water is added to thin down paints). This is extremely helpful for stroke-work designs, such as the Ukrainian-style lap desk on page 14 and the Country-style Game Board on page 60.

PALETTE

There are many different types of commercial palettes available. I like to use a wet palette made with a damp kitchen sponge wrapped in a piece of greaseproof paper or GLAD Bake. The paper allows a small amount of moisture to seep through, and so stops your paints drying out as quickly as they would on a tile or plate. Cleaning up is easier too, as the used paper can be disposed of quickly when it is no longer required, with no washing up. If you do need to go on using the wet palette, store it in an airtight container. This will keep the unused paint from drying out for a couple of weeks.

OTHER ESSENTIALS

In your painting kit for these projects you will also need the following items:

- natural sea sponge
- water jar
- paper towel or rags
- cotton buds (for removing the not-so-great comma strokes!)
- graphite (or transfer) paper in black and white
- kneadable eraser or soft white rubber
- sandpaper in grades 180 and 320
- tack cloth
- ruler or tape measure
- white chalk
- Jo Sonja's Clear Glazing Medium
- Jo Sonja's Flow Medium
- Jo Sonja's Tannin Blocking Sealer
- imitation gold leaf
- cotton gloves
- steel wool, grade 0000
- sponge-filled sanding block
- toothbrush
- wood filler (I use Polyfilla)
- antiquing patina
- artists' oil paints: Burnt Umber and Raw Sienna
- oil-based varnish, satin and gloss finish

TECHNIQUES

PREPARING WOODEN SURFACES

All the items in this book are painted on either pine or MDF (Customwood and Craftwood are the brand names). Before you start painting, remove any hinges or clasps, then fill any nail holes with wood filler. Sand the filler when it is dry. For health reasons, it is a good idea to wear a mask and work in a well-ventilated area when filling and sanding your projects, to avoid breathing in any particles and dust.

BASE COATING

I do not bother to sand my projects before a first coat of base colour (unless the wood is really rough), as I find this first coat of paint raises the grain of the wood and seals it at the same time. I then thoroughly sand all the surfaces, using 320 grade sandpaper, paying special attention to any routered edges. Detailed sanding after this first coat of background colour gives a smooth and sealed surface to continue base coating on. However, if you prefer, you can use a sealer mixed in your first base coat.

Remember to sand your project lightly between each coat of colour.

I have used a 2.5 cm (1") bristle brush to apply all the base coating for the projects in this book. Details for the preparation of each project are given with the instructions for that project.

PLASTIC WRAP MARBLING

This is an easy faux finish that gives extra interest to your work. The finish is applied on top of the base coat, before you transfer the design.

Mix a little water into the colour you will be using for the top coat. The amount of water depends on how dramatic an effect you want; the more water you add, the more transparent and therefore less obvious the finish will be. Test your colours on a sample board before you begin your project. Make sure you have mixed enough colour to finish the whole item as it is difficult to remix exactly the same consistency. Working on one flat surface at a time, use a large brush to cover your article with the diluted top colour. Before it has time to dry, gently press a slightly wrinkled sheet of plastic kitchen wrap onto the wet paint. Lift off the plastic kitchen wrap. This results in a marbled effect.

You can dilute your top coat with Jo Sonja's Clear Glazing Medium instead of water which will produce a different effect. The glazing medium/paint mix will hold the shape of the marbling more obviously than paint mixed with water alone, which tends to give a gentle, washy look. Experiment with both effects on your sample boards to see which finish you prefer.

PAINTING TECHNIQUES

LOADING YOUR BRUSH

When loading the brush in a single colour, the paint needs to be loaded all the way through the bristles, not just on the tip. As a general rule for stroke work, load the paint two-thirds to three-quarters of the way up the brush. Be careful to avoid too much paint building up around the ferrule (the metal part) as this will be difficult to remove and will prevent the bristles from spreading open.

Avoid having excess paint on the brush. If there is so much paint on the brush that the bristles are not visible through the paint, the brush is probably overloaded. The amount of paint on the brush will vary depending on what is being painted, but this is a good guide.

Achieving the right consistency of paint is especially important – it should be the consistency of cream. If it is too runny, puddles will form at the ends of the strokes and you will not be able to paint fine points on the tips. Wispy, ragged tails at the ends of the strokes indicate that the paint is too dry. The more you practise brush strokes, the easier it will be to achieve the right consistency.

HOLDING THE BRUSH

Hold the brush where the ferrule joins the wooden handle. Keep the brush at a relaxed angle, not upright. Rest the side of your hand on your work to give you stability when you are painting and avoid shaky brushwork.

DOUBLE LOADING

Double loading is a method of loading the brush in two colours at the same time. It is not just a matter of dipping the brush into one colour, then another, but rather a controlled method of using two colours together to create gradations from light to dark, or dark to light, with a single stroke.

Load the brush, as normal, in the main colour you are using, then pull your brush carefully across the top of the second colour lifting the paint onto one side of the brush. Avoid just sweeping the tip through the paint, but rather try to get the second colour right along the length of the bristles.

Depending on the effect you are seeking, you can then blend the brush on your palette once or twice for a soft transition of colour or you can use the brush load as it is – especially when you want distinct colour for traditional stroke work.

Double loading works best with fresh paints, so you need to reload the brush frequently.

Put the highlight colour on the palette in a strip, rather than a puddle. You can then load the highlight colour by working down the strip at right angles – this uses much less paint.

BRUSH STROKES

Many styles of folk art are made up of combinations of brush strokes used to form flowers and leaves, decorative borders and other design elements. Brush strokes are the foundation of folk art, and you must be familiar with them, before you begin painting the projects in this book. Practice is the best method of gaining confidence with brush strokes.

Refer to the brush stroke worksheet on page 7 for examples of brush strokes used in the painting of the projects in this book.

- Comma strokes (left-hand side): Place the tip of the brush down pointing to the left-hand corner, and allow

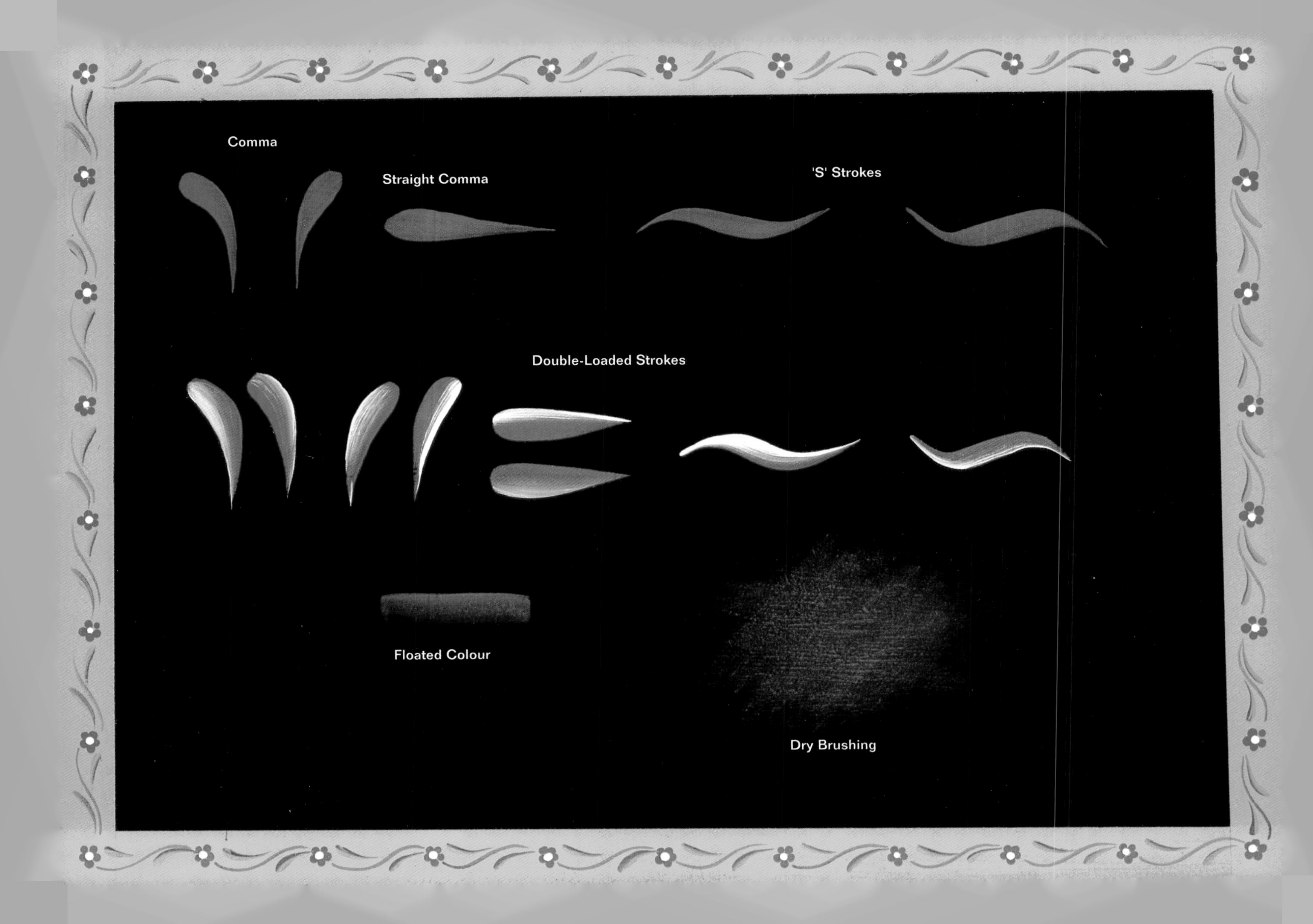
Comma
Straight Comma
'S' Strokes
Double-Loaded Strokes
Floated Colour
Dry Brushing

the bristles to spread out, making the beginning of the stroke rounded. The bigger the stroke, the more pressure is needed on the tip. Gradually pull your fingers in towards your hand, slowly lifting the brush as you do. Keep lifting until the stroke tapers off into a fine tail. The tail of the comma should be directed towards the bottom of the page. Avoid painting sharply angled commas (like golf clubs) or commas that are too curved overall.

• Comma stroke (right-hand side): This is the mirror image of the left-hand side comma stroke. Paint it in the same way, except that the brush points to the right-hand corner. Some people find that rolling the brush can be helpful in achieving a fine tail. If you want to try this, roll the brush by twisting your thumb outwards a quarter turn, as you lift the brush.

• Straight comma stroke: This is painted horizontally. Place the brush down, allowing the bristles to spread out. Pull the brush along, then gradually start to lift it, while you continue to pull. Twist the brush, rolling the thumb outwards a quarter turn, while still gradually lifting it. The stroke should taper from a rounded beginning to a fine point.

• S stroke: This stroke can be painted either horizontally or vertically. Flatten the point of the brush as you load it in paint. Use the side edge of the flattened brush to paint the beginning of the stroke. Apply pressure as you start to change direction, so the centre part of the stroke is much thicker than the beginning. Lift the brush gradually as you change direction for the tail of the stroke. You may find that practising this stroke between two parallel lines is helpful.

• C stroke: When loading the paint onto the brush for this stroke, roll the brush gently to form a point on the tip. Hold the brush vertically and maintain its position throughout the stroke. Use only the tip of the brush to paint the beginning of the stroke and apply more pressure as you get to the centre. Lift the brush to a final point for the tail. Try to move your whole hand when making this stroke, rather than using just your fingers, as this often causes the bristles to fan out of control at the end of the stroke.

HIGHLIGHTING AND SHADING

In some of the projects, I refer to highlighting and shading to add shape to objects that have been base coated. To shade something means adding a dark colour, while highlighting means adding a lighter colour.

Shading and highlighting can be applied by double-loading, dry-brushing or floating. Refer to the individual projects for the placement of shading and highlights, and the appropriate method to use.

FLOATED COLOUR

Floated colour is a way of adding shading to an object using a flat brush, to make it appear three-dimensional.

Load colour only onto one corner of a flat brush, that has previously been loaded in a small amount of water, clear glazing medium or a retarder. Aim for a gentle transition from intense colour through to no colour, across the width of the brush. This is achieved by blending carefully on the palette, after you have loaded some colour, but not yet begun to paint.

Loading the brush in clear glazing medium, I find, gives the best results because, being of a gel consistency, it holds the paint more evenly than water and is easier to keep at the right consistency – not too runny, not too dry.

If you are floating colour on a large area, you can load your brush in a retarder, rather than clear glazing medium, to give you more time to blend your shading.

The lid of the Australiana Picnic Basket on page 24 was speckled before it was antiqued

DRY BRUSHING

Dry brushing is a very simple, yet effective method of shading. Use a dry bristle brush loaded in only a touch of paint. Work the paint into the bristles by dabbing it on a paper towel or rag. Drag the brush lightly over the surface of your painting, following the direction of the shape you are highlighting or shading. You will gradually build up a light 'dusting' of colour. Be patient – it takes a little time

Try to avoid getting blotches of colour as a result of having too much paint on the brush or pushing the brush down too hard on the painting surface.

SPECKLING

Some of the projects, such as the game board on page 60 and the picnic basket on page 24, are 'speckled' before they are antiqued or varnished. This simply involves flicking some slightly diluted paint over the surface of the project.

Use a dampened toothbrush to pick up a little paint, usually Brown Earth or Burnt Sienna. Hold the brush about 20 cm (8 in) above your work with the bristles facing down, then pull your finger over the bristles to flick tiny dots of paint all over your work. The wetter your paint or your toothbrush is, the bigger the dots will be.

You can also dip a piece of sewing cotton in some diluted paint and flick this onto your project to get uneven and random lines here and there. I have used this technique, along with speckling, on the teddy sewing trunk on page 36.

GILDING

There are a few different methods of gilding, or applying gold leaf. The method I have used for the projects in this book is probably one of the simplest, as it uses only Jo Sonja's Tannin Blocking Sealer and imitation gold leaf.

Base coat the area to be gilded with two coats of background colour, sanding lightly between coats. Seal this area with one thin coat of the sealer and allow this to dry. Try not to build up any brush-stroke ridges of sealer, aiming to have the surface as smooth as possible.

Working in sections, apply a second coat of sealer and allow this to dry slightly; this usually takes from three to five minutes.

Wearing cotton gloves to avoid tarnishing the gold leaf, tear the sheets of gold leaf into smaller pieces and press them into the tacky sealer. Overlap the pieces to cover all the background colour, but do not brush off any excess gold leaf at this stage. You can use a soft, dry brush to gently push the gold leaf into hard-to-get-at places. Allow the piece to dry for a couple of hours or overnight, then brush off any overlapping or loose pieces using your hands (wearing your gloves).

If you want your gilding to have an aged look, distress the leaf by rubbing over it with very fine steel wool (0000 grade), then seal it all with another coat of sealer.

If you prefer a smoother look, you can patch any areas to which the gold leaf has not adhered by reapplying the sealer and adding some more gold leaf to the holes, then seal it with a topcoat of sealer. Your project can then be antiqued if you like the gold to have a mellow, rich appearance, or left as it is if you prefer a brighter look.

ANTIQUING

Antiquing your work is a simple process that gives your newly decorated project the appearance of having survived years of handling and use, and disguises the fresh brightness of new paint.

Antiquing involves staining your project with artists' oil paint in any of a variety of different colours, then wiping off the excess paint to leave a tint or a heavy stain, depending on your taste. I antique almost all of my work as I like the old, warm look it gives to the colours.

After your project has completely dried, wipe your work all over with a cloth that has been dipped in a little antiquing patina (antiquing patina is a thinner that dilutes oil paint). Add a tiny amount of oil paint to the same cloth and rub this gently over the project. The amount of paint on the cloth determines how dark the finished look will be. If your work looks too dark, you can wash off some of the antiquing by rubbing it off with more patina on a clean cloth.

I like to darken areas of my work, especially around the edges, to frame the pieces by adding heavy, undiluted oil paint with an old bristle brush, then using a cloth to wipe it over and blend the edges in. This is especially effective with routered or decorative edges as the oil paint gets caught in the grooves and simulates the aged look that appears to come from years of handling.

Before disposing of your used rags, dampen them with water to prevent them igniting in hot weather.

You can use many different colours of oil paint for antiquing, depending on your background colour. I usually use Burnt Umber and occasionally Raw Sienna for pale-coloured backgrounds. Antiquing only colours your work – it doesn't protect it from wear and tear, so you still have to varnish projects with an oil-based varnish.

VARNISHING

As I antique most of my work, I use oil-based varnishes to finish them, as water-based varnishes do not adhere well to the oil-based antiquing media. I like to use Wattle's Instant Estapol or one of the Feast Watson varnishes, as both brands give even, smooth finishes when applied correctly.

I use a 2.5 cm (1") flat synthetic brush to apply the varnish and lightly sand between each coat with an old, worn, sponge-filled sanding block. Wipe the piece with a tack cloth to remove any sanding dust, before applying the next coat of varnish.

For items that look best with a low sheen, varnish them with three coats of satin varnish. Projects with a high gloss finish require more coats – between five and ten coats give a beautiful, even shine.

FRUIT PLATTER

According to fable, the cornucopia, or horn of plenty, was the horn of the goat that suckled Jupiter, and is recognised as an emblem of plenty. A harvest of fruit tumbles out of the cornucopia on this platter, which is framed by a gilded edge.

This method of painting could not be easier, as you simply base paint the fruit shapes, roughly shade and highlight each piece with double-loading, then blend all your shading with dry brushing. All the shadows are added with antiquing to give a dark, rich glow to your platter.

MATERIALS

- Round MFD platter, total diameter 44 cm ($17^1/_4$ in), painting surface 34 cm ($13^1/_2$ in) diameter
- Jo Sonja's Artists Colors: Titanium White, Yellow Oxide, Yellow Light, Napthol Crimson, Diox Purple, Storm Blue, Antique Green, Burnt Sienna, Moss Green, Carbon Black, Raw Sienna
- Round brush, size 3
- Liner brush
- Bristle brush, size 5
- Toothbrush
- Antiquing patina
- Cloth
- Oil paint, Burnt Umber
- Two bristle brushes, size 0 (for antiquing)
- Jo Sonja's Tannin Blocking Sealer
- Cotton gloves
- Imitation gold leaf
- Steel wool, 0000 grade
- Oil-based varnish, gloss
- White graphite paper
- Stylus

PREPARATION

See the painting design on the Pull Out Pattern Sheet and the worksheet on page 13.

STEP ONE

Base paint the platter with two or three coats of Carbon Black, sanding well between coats.

STEP TWO

Transfer the pattern, using the graphite paper and stylus.

Hint: I have used a round brush to base paint and shade all the fruit, however you could use a flat brush, if you find it more comfortable.

PAINTING

CORNUCOPIA

STEP ONE

Base paint the entire cornucopia in Raw Sienna – this will probably take three or four coats. Don't worry if you build up a bit of texture, as this will just make the dry brushing look more interesting.

STEP TWO

Mix up some cream (Titanium White with a touch of Yellow Oxide). Load the round brush in Raw Sienna and double-load it in the cream – be generous with the amount of paint on the brush. Lighten the right side of the horn by painting a long stroke down the edge, keeping the cream towards the outside. Work this in roughly towards the middle of the horn, about one-third of the way. Highlight the same way around the right side of the scroll section of the horn. When this is dry, use your bristle brush to dry-brush more cream over the same areas to soften the highlighting.

STEP THREE

Darken the left side of the horn by loading the round brush in Raw Sienna and double-loading it in Burnt Sienna. Paint this down the left side of the horn and also around the left side of the scroll section. Dry-brush more Burnt Sienna on the dark areas to blend the shading. Dry-brush a little cream into the centre of the inside section of the horn (just above the fruit).

STEP FOUR

Load the round brush in Raw Sienna and add a double load of cream. Paint comma strokes around the rim of the horn, starting the strokes at the lower edge and working from the left side to the right, reloading when necessary. The rest of the shading on the cornucopia is added with antiquing.

APPLES

Base paint the apples in three or four coats of Napthol Crimson. Use the bristle brush to dry-brush some Yellow Oxide onto the right 'shoulder' of the apples. Use slightly curving strokes and avoid the hollow on the apple where the stalk will go. Add some Yellow Light to the brush and intensify this highlight by adding more dry brushing in the centre of the Yellow Oxide.

PEARS

STEP ONE

Base paint the pears in Yellow Oxide, then load the round brush in Yellow Oxide with a double loading of Raw Sienna. Paint a stroke down the dark side of the pear, with the Raw Sienna, towards the outside of the stroke. Work this shading casually towards the centre of the pear.

STEP TWO

Reload the brush in Yellow Oxide and add a double load of cream (Titanium White with a touch of Yellow Oxide). Stroke this down the light side of the pear, working it in towards the middle. Dry-brush Raw Sienna over the dark side, cream on the light side and, finally, Yellow Oxide in the centre to blend the shading together. Dry-brush a tiny touch of Napthol Crimson on the bottom of the dark side of the pear.

PEACHES

Base paint the peaches in a mix of Yellow Oxide, Yellow Light and Titanium White (1:1:1). Mix a touch of Napthol Crimson into some Yellow Light to make orange. Load the round brush in the base colour and double-load it in the orange. Paint a stroke around the outside of the peach, roughly blending the colour in (keep the orange to the outside of the peach). Reload the brush in the same colours and paint them around the top edge of the centre section of the peach. Dry-brush orange on top of the shading to soften the blending. Add some dry brushing in cream to the centre of the front section of the peach.

BLUE PLUMS

Mix some Diox Purple with Storm Blue (1:1), then add a touch of Titanium White. Base paint the plums in this colour. Lighten the base colour with some extra Titanium White. Highlight the top edge of the plum and the top edge of the front section of the plum by loading the brush in the plum colour, then adding a double load of the paler plum colour. Soften the highlighting by dry-brushing some of the paler plum colour over the blending.

GREEN GRAPES

Base paint the grapes in Moss Green, following the outline of each bunch of grapes, then just fill in all the centre of the bunch. Trace the shape of the grapes back on. Highlight the top right of each grape by painting a stroke of Moss Green double-loaded in cream around the edge, keeping the cream to the outside of each grape. Add some dry brushing in cream to the grapes.

LEAVES

STEP ONE

Base paint the leaves in Antique Green. Load the brush in Antique Green, then double-load with Napthol Crimson. Paint a casual stroke along the lower edge of each leaf, keeping the Napthol Crimson to the outer edge. Work this roughly towards the centre of the leaf (about one-third of the way).

STEP TWO

Reload with Antique Green, then double-load in cream. Paint a stroke along the top edge of each leaf, keeping the cream to the outer edge. Work this in towards the middle of the leaf (one-third of the way). Using the bristle brush, dry-brush some of the cream colour onto the light side of the leaves to soften the shading.

Detail of the fruit platter

STALKS

Paint the stalks using the liner brush loaded in Burnt Sienna lightened with a touch of Titanium White.

FINISHING

STEP ONE

Gild the edge of the platter, following the instructions for gilding on page 9. Speckle with Burnt Sienna, using the toothbrush.

STEP TWO

Antique the platter by rubbing a little patina on a cloth all over the plate. Add a smudge of Burnt Umber oil paint to the same cloth and rub over the platter to give a gentle tint of colour.

STEP THREE

Use the oil paint to build up shadows between the fruit by applying undiluted paint with one of the small bristle brushes. Blend out the edge of the shading with the other small bristle brush, wherever one piece of fruit overlaps another. The oil paint 'shadow' should be on the fruit at the back.

Hint: Shading the grapes takes some time and it is difficult to stop some of the antiquing shadows getting onto the grapes in front. I use a cotton bud dipped in a little patina to clean up the edges when I have finished all the shading.

STEP FOUR

Apply a heavy shadow of oil paint on both sides of the rim of the cornucopia. Blend this away from the rim. Add a shadow onto the inside of the horn behind the fruit that is tumbling out.

STEP FIVE

Varnish with four or five coats of gloss varnish – the more coats, the shinier the surface! Use three coats of satin oil-based varnish, if you prefer a less glossy finish.

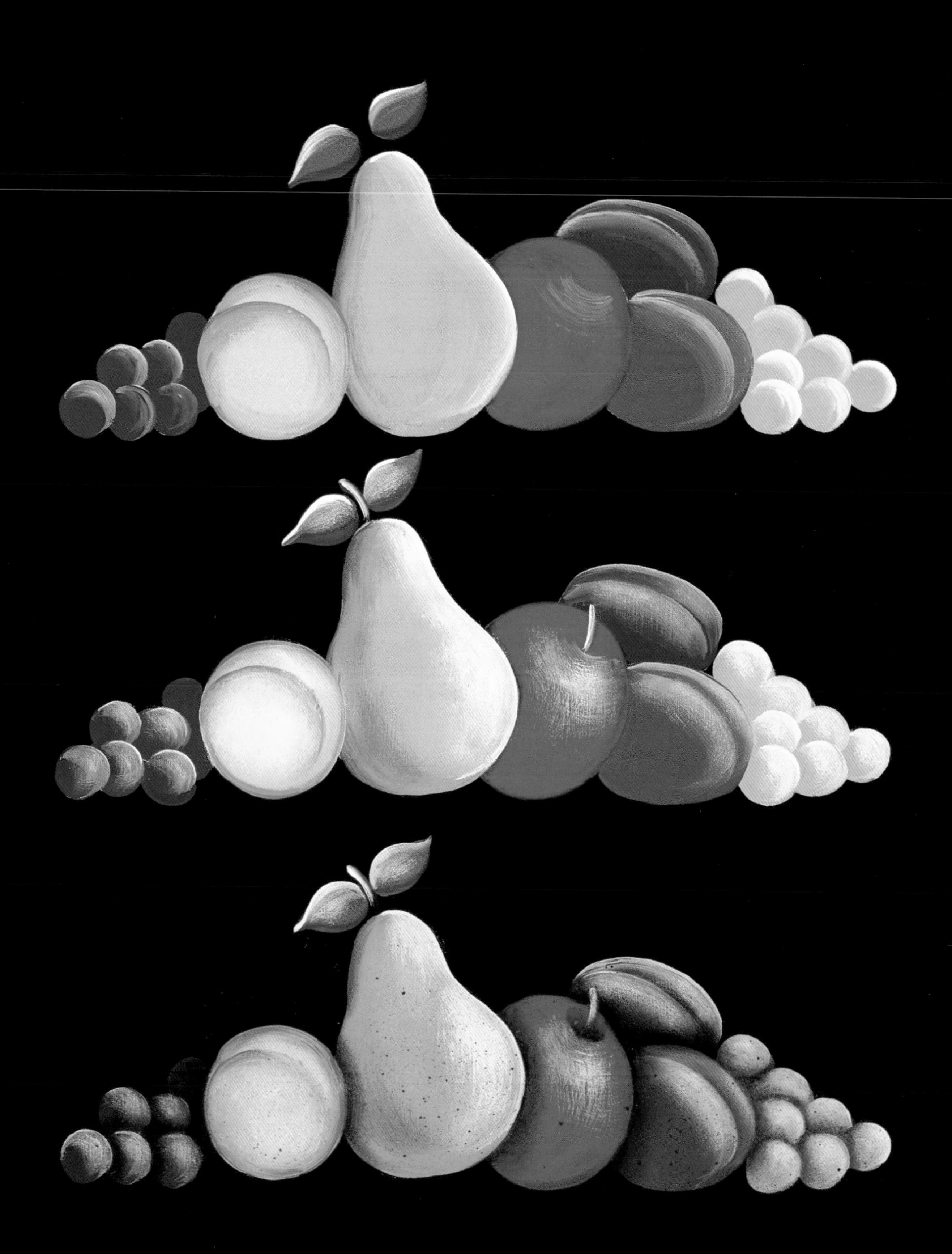

UKRAINIAN-STYLE LAP DESK

Ukrainian folk art has long been a favourite of mine, especially the painting from the Petrikivka region. It's a very stylised, simplistic form of painting, using basic brush strokes to build up flowers and border designs, and appeals to me as I enjoy painting precise, crisp stroke work (especially when I've just got a new brush).

To give this little lap desk an old and treasured look, I have distressed the background as well as the painting. To produce a distressed look, the surface is sanded back, especially in areas that would be most subject to wear and tear. In addition, I have antiqued the whole piece quite heavily. For detailed instructions on antiquing, see page 9.

MATERIALS

Small MDF lap desk, 28 cm x 23.5 cm (11 in x 9 1/4 in)
Jo Sonja's Artists Colors: Carbon Black, Red Earth, Yellow Oxide, Titanium White, Rich Gold, Antique Green, Napthol Red Light
Round brush, size 3
Liner brush
1" bristle brush
Stylus
Steel dressmaker's pin
Scotch Magic Tape
Jo Sonja's Flow Medium
Antiquing patina
Cloth
Oil paint, Burnt Umber
Sandpaper, 320 grade
Ruler
White graphite paper
Oil-based varnish, satin

PREPARATION

See the painting designs on the Pull Out Pattern Sheet and the worksheet on page 17.

STEP ONE

Base paint the lap desk with two or three coats of Red Earth using the bristle brush to build up some texture. Sand lightly between coats. Any brush strokes or ridges of paint will help to give the desk an antique appearance.

STEP TWO

Paint a coat of Carbon Black on the top of the desk. Using the Scotch Magic Tape, mask off a border 1.5 cm (5/8 in) wide around the top and the bottom edges of the sides of the lap desk. Paint these borders in Carbon Black. Sand all the Carbon Black areas well to distress them and reveal some of the Red Earth underneath.

STEP THREE

Paint the outer edge of the lid and the pencil rest in Rich Gold.

STEP FOUR

Transfer the pattern using the graphite paper and stylus.
Hint: Add some flow medium to the paint (two or three drops for each colour) before you start the stroke-work flowers and leaves. The flow medium dilutes the paint a little so the strokes glide on, without being transparent.

PAINTING

FLOWER 1

Load the round brush in Yellow Oxide and add a double load of Titanium White. Starting at the bottom of the flower, paint comma stroke petals, keeping the white towards the lower edge of each stroke. Fill in the centre of the flower in Red Earth. Use the liner brush to paint in long straight commas in Red Earth around the top of the flower, then add some tiny Titanium White straight commas under the Red Earth ones. Paint some fine Rich Gold lines coming up from the base of the Red Earth centre.

FLOWER 2

STEP ONE

Using the round brush loaded in Red Earth and double-loaded generously in Napthol Red Light, start at the base of the flower and paint comma strokes to fill in the centre. Work from the outer edges in towards the middle, keeping the Napthol Red Light facing the outside of the flower for each stroke.

STEP TWO

Add Rich Gold lines coming out from the base of the red centre over the comma strokes. Load the brush in Yellow Oxide, double-loaded in Titanium White and paint commas down the left side of the flower. Reload in the Yellow Oxide and add a double load of Red Earth for the commas on the right side.

STEP THREE

Use Antique Green to paint the stamen lines and add a Titanium White dot to the end of each of the stamens using the head of the pin.

NAKED
and the
DEAD
Norman
Mailer
OF
THE
INLAND
THE
BREAKING
POINT
BY
DAPHNE
DU MAURIER

FLOWER 3

STEP ONE

Paint tiny Red Earth hearts at the top of the flower, using two short straight comma strokes joined together for each heart. Connect these into the centre of the flower with Antique Green stems. Use the liner brush to add three tiny Yellow Oxide strokes to the base of each heart.

STEP TWO

Load the round brush in Red Earth, double-loaded in Napthol Red Light and paint in the main petals of the flower, working from the outside in to the centre. Keep the Napthol Red Light facing towards the outer side of each stroke and reload frequently, so that when the painting is dry, you can see ridges of the Napthol Red Light on each petal.

STEP THREE

Add some Rich Gold overstrokes using the liner brush. The centre of the flower is painted in Yellow Oxide, double-loaded in Red Earth. Keep the Red Earth away from the centre. Use the head of the pin to add Titanium White dots under the centre of the flower. Work from the middle outwards so that the dots become smaller away from the centre. Paint tiny straight comma strokes in Titanium White around the top of the flower, using the liner brush. Using the stylus, add Titanium White dots coming down the stem of each heart.

FLOWER 4

STEP ONE

Paint the stems of these flowers first, using the liner brush loaded in Antique Green. Load the round brush in Yellow Oxide, double-loaded in Red Earth. Paint a comma stroke for the left side of each flower, keeping the Red Earth to the left side of the brush.

STEP TWO

Reload in Yellow Oxide and add a double load of Titanium White. Paint a comma stroke for the right side of each flower, keeping the Titanium White to the right-hand side of the brush. Add some fine Titanium White stamens coming out from each flower, using the liner brush.

LEAVES AND STEMS

STEP ONE

Paint the leaves with comma strokes of Antique Green, double-loaded in Titanium White. Start at the tip of the leaf and work down to the base, keeping the Titanium White on the left side of the brush for the left side of the leaf and on the right for the right side of the leaf. Make sure the comma strokes are painted close together so that none of the background shows through.

STEP TWO

Paint all the stems in Antique Green and the comma leaves in Antique Green, double-loaded in Rich Gold.

CORNER DESIGN

STEP ONE

Base paint the leaves in Antique Green. Mix a little Titanium White into some Antique Green and paint a smaller leaf shape over the original Antique Green. Add a centre vein and outline one side of the leaves in Rich Gold, using the liner brush. Paint all the stem lines in Antique Green and the comma leaves in Antique Green, double-loaded in Rich Gold.

STEP TWO

Load the round brush in Yellow Oxide with a double load of Titanium White. Paint in the strokes on the centre of the flower, keeping the Titanium White on the outside of each stroke. Paint the side petals in the same way as the flower centre. Add some tiny straight comma strokes of Red Earth in the centre of the flower and a Red Earth dot where all the petals meet.

STEP THREE

Use the tip of the round brush to paint three petals of Red Earth on each bud and connect them to their stems with a Rich Gold dot, made using the head of the pin.

STEP FOUR

Paint the Titanium White dot flowers, using the stylus, starting near the base of the stems and working out to the tip.

BORDER PATTERN

Mark off intervals of 2 cm (3/4 in) around the edges of the lid and, on each mark, place a Red Earth dot daisy, made up of five dots in a close circle. Add a Yellow Oxide centre to each daisy, then connect them with a long Titanium White liner brush comma. Use the liner brush to paint three tiny straight comma strokes of Antique Green for the leaves on the outer side of each daisy.

SIDE BORDER PATTERN

STEP ONE

Along the centre of the Red Earth strip, mark off intervals of 2 cm (3/4 in) and paint a dab daisy at each interval. Use the round brush loaded in Yellow Oxide and dipped into some Titanium White to paint five dabs in a circle to form the daisy. Make sure you have lots of paint on the tip of your brush so that the petals stay rounded. Add a Titanium White centre to each of these daisies. Link them with a stem of Antique Green and paint tiny comma leaves of Antique Green, double-loaded in Rich Gold.

STEP TWO

Mark off 2 cm ($^3/_4$ in) intervals on the black edges, above and below the Red Earth strip and paint a long Titanium White comma between these intervals, using the liner brush. Using the pin, add three Red Earth dots where the commas meet, then add a Carbon Black dot on the Red Earth strip, under each join.

FINISHING

STEP ONE

Sand the painting here and there to distress it. Antique the whole desk heavily with Burnt Umber oil paint. Rub a little patina over the desk with a cloth, then add some oil paint to the cloth and wipe this over the box to give a mellow, aged look.

STEP TWO

When all the paint is dry, varnish the lap desk with three coats of varnish.

Detail of the side border and corner patterns

Detail of the centre of the lid

ZHOSTOVA CHOCOLATE BOX

I first came across this style of painting when my brother brought a beautiful book about Zhostova trays back from St Petersburg, five years ago. The trays were mostly lavish floral designs, painted in rich, vibrant colours. As the book was completely written in Russian, I could only look at the pictures, and guess at the methods used to paint the almost translucent designs on the trays. I found out later that they are still being produced in this area of Russia, and that the trays are painted using oil paints and glazes.

This chocolate box is an adaptation of the kinds of slightly stylised flowers used in Zhostova painting. I have tried to re-create the depth in the petals and leaves by using layers of colours, diluted with Jo Sonja's Clear Glazing Medium to build up translucency and subtle shading.

MATERIALS

- Round MDF box, 10 cm (4 in) in diameter and 6 cm (2½ in) high
- Jo Sonja's Artists Colors: Carbon Black, Titanium White, Burgundy, Pine Green, Moss Green, Yellow Light, Raw Sienna, Napthol Red Light, Napthol Crimson, Smoked Pearl, Rich Gold, Pearl White, Burnt Sienna
- Round brush, size 3
- Liner brush
- Flat brush, size 6 or 8
- Filbert brush, size 6 or 8 (optional but very handy!)
- 1" bristle brush
- Jo Sonja's Clear Glazing Medium
- White chalk
- Small stylus
- Plastic kitchen wrap
- White graphite paper
- Oil-based varnish, gloss
- Kneadable rubber or a soft white rubber
- Cloth
- Sandpaper, 320 grade

PREPARATION

See the painting design on page 74 and the worksheet on page 23.

STEP ONE

Base coat the inside and the outside of the chocolate box with two or three coats of Carbon Black, sanding well between coats.

STEP TWO

Marble the outside of the box, using the plastic kitchen wrap and Rich Gold mixed with a touch of Burnt Sienna and the glazing medium (see page 6).

STEP THREE

Paint the rims of the lid and the box with two or three coats of Rich Gold.

STEP FOUR

Transfer the floral pattern (not the border pattern), using the white graphite paper and the stylus. Make sure when you are tracing on the design that you don't press too hard. You only need a faint tracing, otherwise the graphite lines will show through your painting. If your tracing is too bright, rub over it with the kneadable rubber or soft white rubber.

PAINTING

All the flowers and leaves are painted using the same basic method in which a dark colour, mixed with water, is washed all over the shape. A slightly lighter coloured layer (mixed with glazing medium) is then painted over the shape, following the direction of the petals. More layers are added, each being slightly lighter in colour and covering less and less of the shape, so that highlights develop. The outlines and final overstrokes are then added to bring up the final colouring. Subtle tints of contrasting or toning colours can be floated over the finished flowers and leaves to give more interest using a flat brush loaded in glazing medium.

Hint: Before you add any colour to the leaves or petals, paint a coat of glazing medium over the shape, then quickly add the colour (mixed with extra glazing medium) over this before it dries. I use two brushes for this – an old one to apply the glazing medium and a good brush, loaded in the painting colour. This saves time cleaning the brush between coats of glazing medium and paint. The extra coat of wet glazing medium makes the colour glide onto the surface and helps the build-up of colour to appear very smooth.

LEAVES

STEP ONE

Base paint the leaves in watery Pine Green. Have the filbert brush loaded in a little glazing medium, then load it in Pine Green mixed with a touch of Moss Green. Paint the overstrokes, referring to the worksheet for their placement. When they are dry, recoat with a second layer, making these strokes slightly shorter than the first ones, so you do not cover the original strokes completely.

STEP TWO

Add Yellow Light to the previous colour and paint second overstrokes on the lighter side of the leaves, making them slightly smaller than the previous strokes. Strengthen the overstrokes by adding more layers of the light colour – if necessary, drying the box well between each coat.

STEP THREE

Outline the leaves, using the liner, loaded in the Pine Green/Moss Green mix, then add highlight liner work here and there by adding Yellow Light to the Pine Green/Moss Green mix and recoating your liner work on the lighter sides of the leaves. Float Napthol Red Light over the dark side of the leaves close to the vein, using the flat brush.

RED POPPY

STEP ONE

Base paint the shape of the poppy in watery Burgundy. Remember to coat each petal in glazing medium, before you paint every layer. Mix some glazing medium with Napthol Crimson and pull this in from the outer edge of each petal towards the centre of the flower. At this stage, you are not trying to paint individual strokes of colour, but rather trying to build up a fairly solid background of crimson over the petal. Make sure you do not take this colour in all the way to the middle – leave some of the Burgundy showing. Allow to dry, then repaint with a second coat of the Napthol Crimson/glazing medium mix, making this layer slightly shorter than the first. Use Napthol Red Light mixed with glazing medium to strengthen the colour on the petals. Pull this in from the outer edges but do not come into the centre as far as the Napthol Crimson; leave some of this showing. Repeat this step to build up more depth and strength of colour.

STEP TWO

Add a tiny amount of Yellow Light to the Napthol Red Light and paint extra highlights over the petals, referring to the worksheet.

STEP THREE

Paint outlines around the poppy using the liner, loaded in Napthol Red Light first, then highlight these outlines with touches of Yellow Light added to the Napthol Red Light.

STEP FOUR

For the centre, float (with glazing medium) Pine Green mixed with Yellow Light (to make a bright green) in a U shape. When this is dry, add a smaller U in the centre of the first one. Paint the stamens in Yellow Light, using the liner. Add Yellow Light dots and Carbon Black dots around the ends of the stamens.

STEP FIVE

Glaze transparent tints of Yellow Light mixed with Napthol Red Light (to make orange) here and there on the petals.

YELLOW POPPY

STEP ONE

Base paint the poppy in watery Raw Sienna. This poppy is painted using the same method as the red poppy. Use Raw Sienna mixed with a little glazing medium to build up the colour on the petals. Mix some Yellow Light into the Raw Sienna and pull this in from the outer edges of the petals. Build up highlights on the petals by adding a touch of Titanium White to the Yellow Light/Raw Sienna mix and paint small areas of the petals in this mix.

STEP TWO

Paint the liner work on the poppy in Titanium White, mixed with Yellow Light. Glaze transparent touches of orange (Yellow Light/Napthol Red Light) over the petals, here and there. The centre is the same as for the red poppy.

WHITE TULIP

STEP ONE

Base paint the tulip in a watery coat of Pine Green. Use two or three coats of Smoked Pearl mixed with glazing medium to build up the colour on the petals, painting the Smoked Pearl in shorter layers for each coat. Use the flat brush to float the Smoked Pearl on the two side petals.

STEP TWO

Add two or three layers of Titanium White mixed with glazing medium, shortening each layer. Outline the tulip in Smoked Pearl, then highlight the lightest parts of the petals with outlines of Titanium White.

STEP THREE

Float Pine Green around the bottom of the centre and side petals, and above the top edge of the front centre petal, using the flat brush.

STEP FOUR

The centre strokes are painted in Yellow Light, using the liner. Glaze touches of transparent Yellow Light on the petals.

WHITE FLOWERS

STEP ONE

Base paint these flowers in two or three coats of Smoked Pearl mixed with glazing medium, working from the

outer tips of the petals in towards the centre. Strengthen the tips with one or two layers of Titanium White mixed with glazing medium.

STEP TWO

Outline the flowers in Titanium White. Turn the edges of some of the petals in by loading in Smoked Pearl, then double-loading in Titanium White, keeping the white side of the brush facing towards the inside of the petal.

STEP THREE

Glaze some transparent Pine Green over the flower centre. Stipple the centre in Raw Sienna, then paint the stamen in a mix of Napthol Red Light and Pine Green. Add Yellow Light and Titanium White dots.

GRASSES

All the grasses are painted in Napthol Red Light mixed with Pine Green using the liner.

BORDER PATTERN

Note: The Rich Gold paint used in the border pattern does not paint easily over a graphite line so I have found that tracing the design on in chalk is far more successful.

STEP ONE

Rub some white chalk onto the back of the pattern, then align the pattern (right side up) on the box and trace over the design using the stylus to transfer a chalk image.

Hint: If you make any mistakes when you are painting the Rich Gold border, do not try to rub it off as you cannot remove all the metallic particles and they will leave a gold smudge over your work. After the work is dry, paint the background colour over the mistake, then repaint it with the gold.

Detail of the lid design

STEP TWO

Using the liner brush, paint the stems and comma strokes of the pattern. Rub back each section of the chalk design as you come to it with your finger so you can only just see where to paint. Add small dots to the ends of the scrolls with the stylus.

STEP THREE

Use the round brush or filbert brush to paint the daisies in two coats of Pearl White. Add a transparent glaze of Carbon Black to the centre of these daisies, then add four or five tiny dots of Rich Gold with your stylus. Paint the buds in two coats of Pearl White and add a Rich Gold comma to each side of the bud and a dot to join the flower onto the stem.

STEP FOUR

Paint the heart-shaped petals of the gold flowers in Rich Gold with the round brush. When this is dry, use the liner to paint fine Carbon Black lines coming out from the centre of these hearts, making these as tiny and light as you can. Add a Rich Gold dot to the centre of the flower and three dots under the flower. Paint tiny lines above this flower, a long one in the centre, then the other lines, gradually decreasing in size.

FINISHING

When the box is cured (usually about twenty-four hours) remove any chalk lines and dust by wiping the work with a damp cloth. Varnish the box with five coats of gloss varnish and fill it up with delicious chocolates.

AUSTRALIANA PICNIC BASKET

The strong, earthy colours of Australian wildflowers contrast beautifully with the softly sponged and speckled cream background of this wicker picnic basket.

I had the lids made for this basket as I especially liked the pale colour of the wicker, and the basket originally had no lid at all. Most folk art shops can arrange for lids to be made.

MATERIALS

Picnic basket with lid
Jo Sonja's Artists Colors: Titanium White, Yellow Oxide, Antique Gold, Antique Green, Burnt Sienna, Red Earth, Teal Green, Moss Green, Yellow Light, Burgundy, Pine Green
Round brush, size 3
Liner brush
Flat brush, size 8
1/8" deerfoot or stipple brush
1" bristle brush
Jo Sonja's Clear Glazing Medium
Black graphite paper
Stylus
Sea sponge
Toothbrush
Antiquing patina
Cloth
Oil paint, Burnt Umber
Oil-based varnish, satin
Sandpaper, 320 grade

PREPARATION

See the painting design on the Pull Out Pattern Sheet and the worksheet on page 27.

STEP ONE

Remove the lids from the basket and take off any hinges. Base paint the lids in cream (Titanium White mixed with a touch of Yellow Oxide), applying three or four coats, using the bristle brush. Use rough, choppy strokes to give texture to the background and sand lightly between coats.

STEP TWO

Mix some Antique Green with a touch of Burnt Sienna and a touch of Titanium White. Use this to paint the lid edges.

STEP THREE

Use the dampened sea sponge to dab on very watery Antique Green in the area where the painting will go. This will give a fuller look to the foliage. Trace on the first pattern using the black graphite paper and the stylus.

PAINTING

LEAVES

STEP ONE

For the banksia and waratah leaves, base paint them in Teal Green mixed with Pine Green (1:1). Using the liner brush, outline the leaves, then fill in the centres using the round brush. When this is dry, load the flat brush with the glazing medium and side-load it in Moss Green. Float the Moss Green along the top edge of the leaves, then add a float of the same colour under the centre vein.

STEP TWO

For the gum leaves, load the round brush in Antique Green, then dip the tip of the brush into some Burnt Sienna and some Titanium White. Vary the amount of brown and white as you paint the gum leaves. Paint the leaves using long straightish comma strokes, working from the base of the leaf out towards the tip. Add stems and centre veins using the liner brush loaded in a watery mix of Antique Green and Burnt Sienna. Thin the stem colour with water and add wash gum leaves and stems in between the solid ones. These are not marked on the pattern – just add them where you feel they will look good.

Hint: When you are painting wash leaves, work quickly and use as few strokes as possible to fill out the shape, so that you don't get 'overlap' lines down the leaves. Make sure to roll any excess paint off your brush before you start, to avoid making puddles at the ends of your strokes.

BANKSIA

STEP ONE

Use the deerfoot brush to stipple (or lightly dab) Yellow Oxide over the whole shape of the banksia. When this first coat is dry, add some Red Earth to the Yellow Oxide on the brush and stipple a dark centre at the top of the flower and some shading down the right side. Reload the brush in Yellow Oxide and add a little Titanium White. Stipple this around the front edge of the dark centre and down the left side of the flower.

STEP TWO

Use the liner brush loaded in Yellow Oxide, then dipped in Titanium White to add small comma strokes around the edge of the dark centre. Keep these lightest on the left side of the flower. Paint long commas around the base of the banksia, all coming in towards the centre of the base.

WARATAH

STEP ONE

Using the round brush, base paint all the petals and the centre of the flower in Red Earth, then retrace the details of the petals that have been obscured. Pull light, wispy strokes of Burgundy out from the base of the flower onto the lower petals, and add Burgundy shading between the petals in the centre, in the same way. Refer to the worksheet for the placement of the Burgundy shading on the folded petals.

STEP TWO

Add a little Titanium White to the Red Earth and lighten the outer tips of the petals, working in towards the base of the petal. Mix some extra Titanium White into the pale Red Earth and highlight the tips again, leaving some of the first highlight colour showing. Outline each of the petals, using the liner loaded in Titanium White mixed with a touch of Red Earth.

STEP THREE

Paint some tiny comma strokes at the very top of the inner section of the waratah, using the liner brush loaded in Red Earth, then dipped in Titanium White. Lengthen these commas in the middle of the flower.

GUM FLOWERS

STEP ONE

Trace on the second pattern. Use the deerfoot brush to stipple some Red Earth over the gum flowers. Load the liner in Red Earth and paint some fine lines over the stippling, working from the top edge of the flower down and extending slightly over the lower edge. Add some Yellow Oxide to the Red Earth and add more lines on one side of the flower.

STEP TWO

Paint the cap of the flower in Burnt Sienna. When this is dry, double-load the brush in Titanium White and paint a small highlight on the cap on the light side of the flower, keeping the Titanium White to the outer side of the cap.

STEP THREE

Paint the stems of the gum flowers, using the liner brush loaded in Burnt Sienna with a double load of Titanium White. Add some tiny dots of Yellow Oxide and some Titanium White dots around the lower edge of the flower.

GUM NUTS

STEP ONE

Base paint the nuts using the flat brush loaded in Burnt Sienna. When this is dry, dip one side of the flat brush into some Titanium White and the other side into Burnt Sienna. Blend this well to get a smooth transition of colour, then paint a highlight along the upper edge of the nut.

STEP TWO

Paint the stems of the gumnuts in the same way as the stems of the gum flowers.

OVENS EVERLASTING

STEP ONE

Load the tip of the round brush heavily in Titanium White and pull in short strokes for the petals of the flowers and buds. Reload the brush frequently to keep the petals rounded.

STEP TWO

Use the deerfoot brush to stipple some Moss Green in the centre of the flowers. While this is still wet, dip the long edge of the brush into a little Burgundy. Stipple this on the lower edge of the centre. Clean the brush quickly, reload in Moss Green, then dip the long edge of the brush into Titanium White. Stipple this on the top edge of the centre.

STEP THREE

Paint the stems in Teal Green and add a small Teal Green calyx to the buds.

WATTLE

Stipple some Antique Gold wattle using the deerfoot brush. Reload the brush in Yellow Light and stipple more wattle. Add some Titanium White to the long edge of the deerfoot brush (still loaded in Yellow Light) and dab on a highlight to one side of each of the Yellow Light wattle blossoms.

FILLER LEAVES

Load the round brush in Teal Green mixed with Pine Green (1:1). Double-load for some leaves in Moss Green and for others in Titanium White. Place these leaves in any gaps, keeping them close to the centre line.

FINISHING

STEP ONE

Replace the hinges, then speckle the painted lids with Burnt Sienna, using the toothbrush.

STEP TWO

Antique the basket lids by rubbing the cloth dampened with antiquing patina all over them. Add a tiny smudge of Burnt Umber oil paint to the same cloth and wipe over the lids to give a gentle, mellow tone. Intensify the antiquing around the edge of the basket and around the hinges by applying more oil paint with a bristle brush, then blending the paint out with the cloth.

STEP THREE

When the paint is thoroughly dry, varnish with three coats of varnish.

PARTRIDGE PLATE

The stroke-work border and casually 'dabbed' rims, combined with a Smoked Pearl background, give this plate a ceramic look. It's an easy project that will look great hanging on the wall of a kitchen or living area.

MATERIALS

Round MDF plate, total diameter 32 cm ($12^{1}/_{2}$ in), centre painting surface 15 cm (6 in) diameter
Jo Sonja's Artists Colors: Smoked Pearl, Teal Green, Storm Blue, Yellow Oxide, Raw Sienna, Brown Earth, Carbon Black, Warm White, Burgundy
Round brush, size 3
Liner brush
Bristle brush, size 4 or 5
1" bristle brush for base painting
Sandpaper, 320 grade
Black graphite paper
Stylus
Sea sponge
Oil paint: Raw Sienna, Burnt Umber
Antiquing patina
Oil-based varnish, satin

Detail of the rim of the plate

PREPARATION

See the painting design on page 73 and the worksheet on page 31.

STEP ONE

Base coat with two coats of Smoked Pearl, sanding well between coats.

STEP TWO

Transfer the pattern to the centre of the plate, using the black graphite paper and stylus.

STEP THREE

Roughly mix some Warm White with the same amount of Storm Blue and add a touch of Raw Sienna. Don't combine the colours completely, but rather let the brush do the mixing as the colour is applied. Use the bristle brush to paint the middle ring of the plate with this colour. Don't worry if it looks a little streaky as this will add to the casual look. When the paint is dry, distress this blue ring by sanding it until you are happy with the aged appearance (the more sanding the better).

STEP FOUR

Using the bristle brush again, wash on some watery Storm Blue halfway around one side of the centre section of the plate. While this is still wet, quickly dab off the middle of this wash with a clean, damp sponge so that the Storm Blue is less intense towards the middle of the plate. Don't worry if some of the wash goes over the tracing. Repeat this on the other side of the centre of the plate, using Raw Sienna instead of Storm Blue.

PAINTING

PARTRIDGES

STEP ONE

Using the round brush, follow the numbering on the pattern to paint the sections in order. All the areas are based in first, then the details and shading are added later.

- Section 1: Paint the tail feathers in a rough mix of Yellow Oxide and Warm White. When dry, recoat with the same mix double-loaded in Raw Sienna. Keep the Raw Sienna to the under edge of each feather.
- Section 2: Base paint in a mix of Brown Earth and Carbon Black (1:1). Paint the legs in the same colour.
- Section 3: Paint in a rough mix of Yellow Oxide and Warm White. When dry, add a touch of Raw Sienna to the same brush and roughly stroke on a little shading under the wings.
- Section 4: Base paint these areas in Teal Green mixed with Warm White (1:1). Base in the main area first, then use the tip of the brush to flick a wispy edge down onto the pale yellow section of each bird's tummy. Also flick this green over the top of the tail feathers and the dark brown section of the backs. Add a little Teal Green to the brush and darken the lower edge of each bird's tummy.
- Section 5: Paint this area in Yellow Oxide roughly mixed with Warm White, flicking the lower edge over the green on the backs.
- Section 6: Base in Raw Sienna, again flicking the lower edge over the yellow in the backs.

• Section 7: Paint this area in a mix of Burgundy and Raw Sienna (1:1).
• Section 8: Base paint the wings in a rough mix of Yellow Oxide and Warm White.
• Section 9: Paint each bird's head in Teal Green, and the wattle in Raw Sienna with a touch of Burgundy. Darken the wattle colour (by adding extra Burgundy) to paint the wattle on the far side of the heads. The area around the eyes is painted in Brown Earth mixed with a little Carbon Black. Add a dot of Raw Sienna for each eye, then place a smaller dot of Carbon Black in the centre of each eye for the pupil. Paint the partridge's beak in Yellow Oxide.

STEP TWO

Use the bristle brush to dry-brush a cream colour (Warm White mixed with a touch of Yellow Oxide) onto areas 3, 5 and 8. Brush this colour onto the front section of the wattle. Add a little Burgundy to the same brush and dry-brush a highlight onto each partridge's chest (area 7). Clean and dry the brush, then dry-brush a mix of Warm White with a touch of Teal onto all the green areas (including the heads).

STEP THREE

Paint a Warm White band around the throat of each bird, using the liner brush. Outline the beaks, backs and tail feathers in Brown Earth. Load the round brush in Yellow Oxide and dip the tip in some Brown Earth. Paint quick strokes on the tip of the wings, lifting the brush as you pull it along to produce a feathery look. Add more of these strokes to the tail feathers and on the backs and chests.

Detail of the painted partridges in the centre of the plate

BORDERS

STEP ONE

Using the round brush, casually paint slanted strokes of watery Burgundy mixed with a little Raw Sienna around the centre rim of the plate.

STEP TWO

Using the round brush, paint upright dabs of watery Storm Blue around the outer rim. Divide the outer band of the plate into eight sections and paint a stroke-work flower in each section. Use Teal Green for the stems and leaves, Raw Sienna for the inner petals and Burgundy for the outer petals. Keep all these colours a little on the runny side to get a slight transparency in the brush stokes.
Hint: Make sure you do not overload your brush when working with watery paints. To avoid getting drips and puddles at the end of your strokes, roll the excess paint off your brush onto the palette, before you start to paint.

FINISHING

STEP ONE

Sand the border patterns to give a distressed look. Spatter with Brown Earth. Antique the plate by rubbing it lightly all over with the cloth dipped in antiquing patina. Add a little Raw Sienna to the cloth and rub over the plate again. Emphasise the inner rim of the plate by brushing Burnt Umber oil paint heavily around it and blending this away from the rim.

STEP TWO

When all the paint is dry, varnish with three coats of satin varnish.

NAIVE STILL LIFE – BOWL OF PEARS

I love American naive art. The childlike simplicity of the portraits and still life works really appeals to me. I have tried to capture a little of that look in this project and its partner, Still Life with Cherries on page 56.

MATERIALS

Pine frame and backing board, total measurement 40 cm (15$^3/_4$ in) wide x 36 cm (14 in) high, painting surface is 26 cm x 22 cm (10$^1/_4$ in x 8$^3/_4$ in)
Jo Sonja's Artists Colors: Raw Sienna, Yellow Light, Antique Gold, Warm White, Pine Green, Teal Green, Indian Red Oxide, Yellow Oxide, Burnt Sienna, Rich Gold
Bristle brush, size 4 or 5
Round brush, size 3
Liner brush
Toothbrush
Oil paint, Burnt Umber
Antiquing patina
Cloth
Two additional bristle brushes, size 0 (for antiquing)
Langridge Artist Colours Crackle Varnish
Jo Sonja's Clear Glazing Medium
Oil-based varnish, satin
Black graphite paper
Stylus
Sandpaper, 320 grade

PREPARATION

See the painting design on page 76 and the worksheet on page 35.

STEP ONE

Remove the backing board from the frame and base paint it with three to four smooth coats of Warm White, sanding well between coats.

STEP TWO

Transfer the pattern using the black graphite paper and stylus. Do not trace the leaves or stalks on at this stage as they will only be in the way when you are painting the background.

PAINTING

BACKGROUND

Paint the background (behind the bowl) in a mixture of Pine Green and Teal Green (1:1). Paint a 'halo' roughly around the edge of the pears, using the bristle brush loaded in the Pine Green/ Teal Green mix, then dipped in Antique Gold. Use rough, choppy strokes in different directions to lighten the background close to the pears and gradually fade the halo off into the background. Increase the amount of green on the brush and lessen the Antique Gold as you work away from the pears. Touch up the edges of the pears with Warm White if any Antique Gold has been painted on them.

LEAVES

STEP ONE

Trace on the leaves and stalks. Base paint the leaves in the Pine Green/Teal Green mix. Load the round brush in the green mix, then double-load in Indian Red Oxide. Paint a casual stroke along the lower edge of each leaf, keeping the Indian Red Oxide to the outer edge. Work this roughly in towards the centre of the leaf (about one-third of the way).

STEP TWO

Mix a little Yellow Oxide into some Warm White (to make cream). Reload with the Pine Green/Teal Green mix, then double-load in cream. Paint a stroke along the top edge of each leaf, keeping the cream to the outer edge. Work this in towards the middle of the leaf, one-third of the way. Dry-brush some of the cream onto the light side of the leaves to soften the shading, using the bristle brush.

TABLECLOTH

Mix a little Warm White into the Pine Green/Teal Green mix to make a slightly lighter green and paint all the green checks. Use the liner to neaten the corners of the checks. Highlight the green checks by dry-brushing a little Antique Gold onto each intersection, using the bristle brush. Mix a little Warm White into the green check colour and use this to shade the lower left-hand corner of the white checks. Use the liner brush, loaded in Indian Red Oxide, to paint on the detail lines dividing the white squares of the tablecloth.

BOWL

STEP ONE

Base paint the front of the bowl in Warm White, mixed with a touch of the Pine Green/Teal Green mix. Darken this colour by adding a little more green to paint the inner back edge of the bowl that is showing. Paint the upper rim of the bowl in Warm White. Shade the right side of the bowl by loading the round brush in the bowl colour, then double-loading it in the darker shade. Paint a stroke down the

right edge and gradually work the colour in towards the centre of the bowl (about one-third of the way). Shade under the rim of the bowl, in the same way, and also on the base of the bowl.

STEP TWO

Using the liner brush, paint dashes of Pine Green/Teal Green mix along the rim of the bowl. Dry-brush some Warm White onto the centre of the bowl, using the bristle brush, then brush some of the darker shade colour onto the right side of the bowl.

LIGHT PEARS

STEP ONE

Base the light pears in a mix of Yellow Oxide, Yellow Light and Warm White (1:1:1). Shade them by loading the brush in the light pear colour, then double-loading it in Yellow Oxide. Stroke this colour down the left side of the pears (where visible) keeping the Yellow Oxide to the outside. Work this in casually towards the centre.

STEP TWO

Highlight the other side of the pears (where visible), using the light pear colour, double-loaded in cream (Warm White plus a touch of Yellow Oxide). Soften the shading on the pears by dry-brushing them, using the bristle brush. Brush Yellow Oxide on the dark side, cream on the light side and the original base colour in the centre.

DARK PEARS

STEP ONE

Base paint the dark pears in Yellow Oxide. Shade these pears in the same way as the light pears, using Yellow Oxide double-loaded in Raw Sienna on the left side of the pears.

STEP TWO

Add highlights to the right side, using Yellow Oxide double-loaded in the light pear colour (Yellow Oxide, Yellow Light and Warm White 1:1:1). Dry-brush Raw Sienna on the dark side, then add a touch of Indian Red Oxide. Dry-brush some of the light pear colour on the right side. Finally, soften the centre of the pear by brushing on some Yellow Oxide.

STALKS

Use the liner brush to paint the stalks in Burnt Sienna, lightened with a touch of Warm White.

FRAME

STEP ONE

Sand the frame well, then paint it with a mixture of the glazing medium and Warm White (1:1). When this is dry, sand again, then add a second coat.

STEP TWO

Add a little Warm White to the Teal Green/Pine Green mix. Paint a thin coat of this on the middle rim of the frame. Don't worry if this looks a bit streaky, it just means less sanding later! When this is thoroughly dry, distress the colour by sanding it back.

FINISHING

STEP ONE

Using the toothbrush, speckle the board with Brown Earth. Antique the picture by applying a little patina onto the cloth and rubbing all over the board. Add a smudge of Burnt Umber oil paint to the same cloth and rub over the picture to give a gentle tint of colour. Darken the corners by adding extra paint to the corners with the large bristle brush and blending in towards the centre with the cloth. Use the oil paint to build up shadows between the pears by applying undiluted paint with one of the small bristle brushes and blending out the edge of the shading with the other small bristle brush, wherever one pear overlaps another. The oil paint 'shadow' should be on the back pear. Add shadows to the leaves behind the pears and on the bowl behind the front pear. Also shade the bowl under the rim and above the rim onto the fruit. Add a shadow on the table from the bowl and another above the crease in the tablecloth.

STEP TWO

If a crackled finish is desired, when the oil paint is completely dry, paint on a coat of the Crackle Varnish Part 1. When this first coat has almost dried, between fifteen minutes and an hour depending on conditions, apply a coat of Part 2. If no cracks have appeared after twenty-four hours, gently warm the surface with a hairdryer. Fine cracks will appear and these can be emphasised by rubbing some slightly diluted Burnt Umber oil paint into them, when the varnish is completely dry.
Hint: This crackle method works better on smooth surfaces than textured paint. Coating your painting with three layers of varnish, before applying the crackle varnish, helps even out the surface and also allows you to wash off the crackle if you are not happy with the result, without disturbing your painting.

Detail of the painted pears

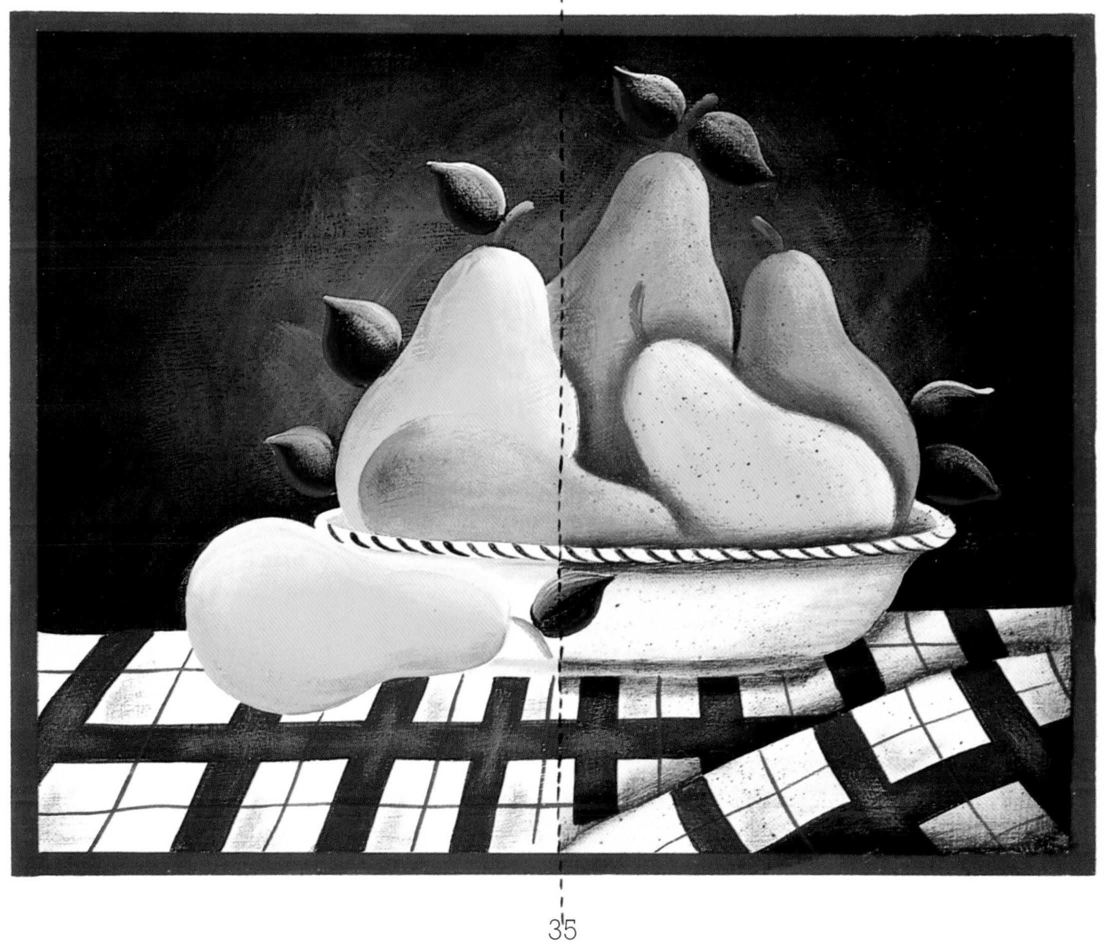

TEDDIES ON A SMALL TRUNK

If you are like me, you probably have plastic bags of knitting, embroidery and sewing scattered around the house. This box is the solution.

MATERIALS

Small MDF trunk, 51 cm (20 in) long, 36 cm (14¼ in) wide and 22 cm (8¾ in) deep
Jo Sonja's Artists Colors: Warm White, Yellow Oxide, Raw Sienna, Burnt Sienna, Brown Earth, Provincial Beige, French Blue, Storm Blue, Burgundy, Red Earth, Carbon Black, Smoked Pearl
Round brush, size 3
Liner brush
1" bristle brush or an old pastry brush
Black graphite paper
Sandpaper, 320 grade
Heavy cotton thread
Stylus
Toothbrush
Chalk pencil
Antiquing patina
Cloth
Oil paint, Burnt Umber
Scotch Magic Tape
Ruler
Oil-based varnish, satin

PREPARATION

See the painting design on the Pull Out Pattern Sheet and the worksheets on pages 40–41.

STEP ONE

Use the bristle brush or the old pastry brush to base coat the trunk, inside and out, with two rough coats of Warm White, sanding well between coats. Aim to have some brush strokes and texture showing in your base painting as this will help to make the trunk look old and loved when it is finished.

STEP TWO

Paint a final coat of Warm White roughly mixed with Yellow Oxide (2:1) all over the box and lid, using the brush to blend the colours on the surfaces rather than mixing the colour to a pale yellow on your palette before you start. This will give an uneven background colour that is more interesting than a flat colour.

STEP THREE

Brush-mix one coat of French Blue and Smoked Pearl over the inside of the box. Distress this lightly by rubbing with sandpaper.

STEP FOUR

Transfer the pattern (except for the lettering) to the lid of the trunk, using the graphite paper and the stylus.

PAINTING

LID BORDER AND STRIPES

STEP ONE

Using the Scotch Magic Tape, mask off the 3.5 cm (1½ in) border around the top edge of the lid. Paint this border and the hearts in each corner in a slightly watery Burgundy, mixed with Red Earth (1:1). Add a fine, liner-brush line of the same colour just inside the border. Sand the border and the hearts lightly to distress them.

STEP TWO

Use the chalk pencil and ruler to mark off 3 cm (1¼ in) stripes around the sides of the box. Paint these stripes freehand in the same colour as the top border, then sand them lightly.

STEP THREE

Transfer the lettering to the border, then paint it with the round brush and pale yellow (Yellow Oxide mixed with Warm White).

TABLE

Mix some Burgundy with some Red Earth (1:1) and use the round brush to casually paint this colour under the bears. Before it has time to dry, clean the brush, then use it (damp) to wash out the lower edge of the shading.

TEDDY BEARS

Note: These bears are painted using the same three-step method as the bear on the photo album on page 64. Begin by base painting the bears in three tones, then add a second coat, blending the tones together at their edges. Finally, add the fine bristles with the liner brush. Refer to the instructions and worksheet for the album before you start.

GIRL BEAR

STEP ONE

Use Burnt Sienna as the darkest colour, Raw Sienna as the medium colour and cream (Warm White mixed with a Yellow Oxide) as the lightest colour for the fur. Paint the first two coats, before adding the clothes, eyes, nose, cotton reel and the fur.

STEP TWO

Base paint the dress in two or three coats of Smoked Pearl. When it is dry, paint some shadows on the folds of the

a stitch in time
in time saves nine

material in Provincial Beige by adding some slightly runny paint down one side of each fold and under the arm, then washing out the edge of the shading before it dries, with the cleaned, damp brush. Highlight the other side of the folds by painting on some Warm White and washing it out the same way. If you prefer, you could float these colours on with a flat brush. Add a little Provincial Beige to the back of the dress where it folds around at the back and highlight right along the top edge of it with Warm White. Paint the shoulder strap with the round brush loaded in Smoked Pearl and double-loaded in Warm White. Wash some watery Smoked Pearl over the dress frill, then outline the frill with Warm White. Add tiny lines along the frill using the liner brush. Use the stylus to add groups of three small dots in Warm White to the dress.

BOY BEAR

STEP ONE

The boy bear is painted using Brown Earth as the darkest shade, Burnt Sienna as the medium shade and Provincial Beige for the lightest colour. Again, paint the first two layers, then the vest, eyes, nose and sewing basket before painting the detail of the fur.

STEP TWO

Paint the vest in two or three coats of French Blue mixed with a little Smoked Pearl. Paint the ribbing around the armholes, the neck and the tummy in straight French Blue. Add fine, liner-brush lines of Storm Blue to the ribbing, then outline all the ribbing, in a paler French Blue than the vest, by adding more Smoked Pearl to the colour.

STEP THREE

Mark on the Fair Isle pattern with a chalk pencil – make it as elaborate or as simple as you like. Paint the different triangles, stripes and lines in a variety of Storm Blue, Smoked Pearl plus Storm Blue, Burgundy and Warm White. Add a little shading to the left side of the vest by painting on some watery Storm Blue and washing out the inner edge of the shading before it dries.

Detail of the teddies on the trunk

BASKET

STEP ONE

Base paint the basket in two or three coats of Smoked Pearl. Shade some watery Provincial Beige under the top rim and above the lower rim and wash out the shading to blend it as it comes in towards the centre of the basket. Use the round brush to add comma strokes of Smoked Pearl, double-loaded in Provincial Beige along the top and bottom edges of the basket.

STEP TWO

Transfer the stroke-work design to the basket. Using the round brush loaded in equal parts of Burgundy and Red Earth, paint the heart, flowers and leaves. When this is dry, sand it lightly to give a 'worn' look.

STEP THREE

Base paint the spool of the cotton reels in pale yellow (Yellow Oxide mixed with Warm White), then paint the side rim of the spool in a slightly darker yellow. Add a Raw Sienna hole in the centre of the spools and outline the back of the spool in Raw Sienna, using the liner brush. Add tiny vertical lines of Raw Sienna around the rims.

STEP FOUR

The pink cotton is painted in Burgundy mixed with Smoked Pearl, with a little Burgundy shading being washed out on the left side near the bear's arm. Add lines of Burgundy running around the dark side of the cotton and pale pink lines of crosshatching on the light side of the spool.

STEP FIVE

Use Yellow Oxide mixed with Warm White for the yellow cotton, making the colour a little darker than the spool itself. Shade some Raw Sienna under the top rim of the spool on the cotton, then add some Raw Sienna cross-hatching on the left side.

STEP SIX

Base paint the blue wool in French Blue mixed with Smoked Pearl. Shade the lower side of the ball in watery French Blue, washing the upper edge of the shading out to blend it roughly. Load the brush in the base colour and dip the tip of the brush into some Smoked Pearl. Casually stroke this two or three times around the top right-hand edge of the ball to lighten it. Add cross-hatching of pale French Blue (base colour plus Smoked Pearl) and use the liner to paint the trailing tail of the wool in this pale French Blue.

STEP SEVEN

The pink ball is based in Burgundy mixed with Smoked Pearl. When this is dry, shade the lower area (between the cotton spool and the rust-coloured ball of wool) with watery Burgundy, washing out the top edge to soften the shading. Highlight the top edge of the ball the same way as the blue ball, using the base colour dipped in Smoked Pearl, then add Burgundy crosshatching.

STEP EIGHT

The rust-coloured balls of wool are painted in a mixture of equal parts of Red Earth and Burgundy with enough Smoked Pearl added to lighten the colour. Darken the lower edge of the ball with Red Earth mixed with Burgundy and blend out the upper edge of the shading. Lighten the top of both of the balls the same way as the blue ball. Use the liner brush to add some Red Earth/Burgundy cross-hatching and some pale Red Earth/ Burgundy crosshatching.

PINCUSHION

STEP ONE

Base paint the lower parts in Yellow Oxide and the top part in Yellow Oxide with some Warm White added. Darken the bottom by painting on some watery Raw Sienna and washing out the top edge of this shading to blend it. Add small watery circles of Raw Sienna at the point where each pin goes into the pincushion.

STEP TWO

Paint the braid around the edge in Smoked Pearl double-loaded in Warm White, using tiny comma strokes lying one next to the other. Paint a knot of Smoked Pearl at each corner and add a liner-brush tassel at each knot. Using the liner brush loaded in dark grey (Carbon Black mixed with a touch of Warm White), paint the pins. Paint a variety of different-coloured dots for the pin heads. Paint a tiny cross in Raw Sienna at the point where the pins enter the pincushion.

FINISHING

STEP ONE

Speckle the project with Brown Earth. Dip a piece of heavy cotton thread into some watery Brown Earth and drop this onto the painting to create dark brown lines here and there.

STEP TWO

Antique the lid of the box lightly by wiping it with a cloth dipped in some antiquing patina, then adding some Burnt Umber oil paint to the same cloth and gently rubbing this over the surface to give a slight brown tint. Make sure not to darken the bears too much. Antique the rest of the box (inside and out) the same way but add stronger colour. Intensify the antiquing around the edges of the box even more by adding extra paint and blending out the edges of the paint with the cloth.

STEP THREE

When all the paint is completely dry, varnish the trunk with three coats of satin varnish.

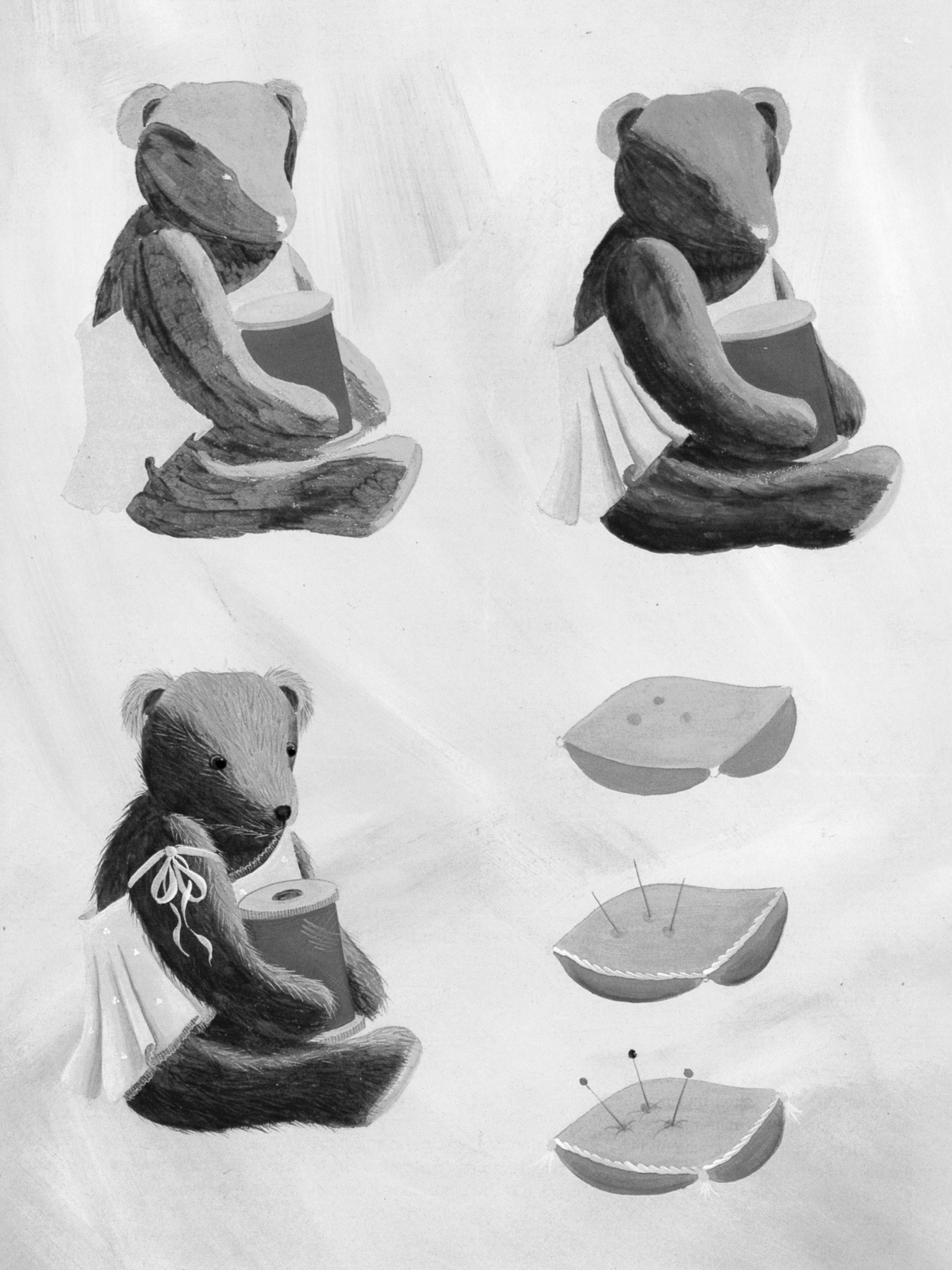

GOLD LACE AND PANSY BOWL

Pansies are my favourite flowers. I have given gold edges to their petals and painted them on a dark background which highlights the richness of the gold lacework.

MATERIALS

Round, lidded powder bowl, 16 cm ($6^1/_4$ in) diameter
Jo Sonja's Artists Colors: Carbon Black, Indian Red Oxide, Titanium White, Rich Gold, Yellow Oxide, Burgundy, Diox Purple, Pine Green, Opal
Round brush, size 3
Liner brush
Stylus
Plastic kitchen wrap
Base-painting brush
1" bristle brush
Sea sponge
Oil paint, Burnt Umber
White graphite paper
Stylus
Antiquing patina, gloss
Cloth
Oil-based varnish, gloss

PREPARATION

See the painting design on page 75 and the worksheet on page 45.

STEP ONE

Base paint the inside of the lid and the bowl in three coats of Titanium White, sanding well between coats. Sponge some watery Rich Gold over the Titanium White.

STEP TWO

Base paint the outside of the bowl in Carbon Black. When the paint is dry, marble, using the plastic kitchen wrap and Indian Red Oxide (see page 6).

STEP THREE

Transfer the pattern lightly, using the white graphite paper and stylus. Be very careful doing this as any stray lines will show through the lacework. **Hint:** If you are using a different-sized bowl, divide the bowl into four sections and transfer the pansy section of the pattern only, then adjust the lacework to fit by adding more scallops or leaving some out so the design exactly fits your bowl.

PAINTING

LACEWORK

Note: When working with metallic paints, do not try to wash off any mistakes as you will leave a glittery residue, but rather let your mistake dry, cover it carefully with the background colour, then repaint.

STEP ONE

Make a wash of Rich Gold by adding water to the paint, then paint in the shape of the scallops. Use the liner, or the flattened tip of the round brush to add fine vertical lines on top of these scallops. Make these lines slightly stronger than the wash but still do not use full-strength paint.

STEP TWO

Using the liner brush, paint the heart shapes between each scallop in two or three coats of Rich Gold so that they stand out. Add three tiny straight comma strokes of Rich Gold to the lower edge of each scallop and three above the middle of each heart.

STEP THREE

With the stylus, add the dots to the lacework, referring to the worksheet. Start in the centre of each scallop and work outwards so that the dots become smaller as they move away from the centre. Add the dots between the groups of pansies on the lid, reloading the brush for each dot so they will all be the same size.

LEAVES

Paint all the leaves, using the round brush loaded in Pine Green, then double-loaded in Rich Gold. Use short, straight comma strokes for the pansy leaves and fine comma strokes for the filler leaves.

PANSIES

There are three different-coloured pansies in the design. The following instructions refer to the top pansy in each group; the other pansies are painted the same way, but in different colours.

YELLOW AND PINK PANSIES

STEP ONE

Base paint the top two petals in two coats of pale yellow (Yellow Oxide with a touch of Titanium White). Reload the round brush in pale yellow and double-load it in a generous amount of Rich Gold. Push out dabs of colour around the edge of one petal (with the gold towards the outside) and quickly pull in the Rich Gold towards the centre of the flower. Reload and repeat this on the other petal. Emphasise the inner side of this second petal by pulling down some extra gold on the edge that overlaps the first petal.

LORENZY
PALANCA
PARIS

STEP TWO

Base paint the two side petals in two coats of pale pink (Burgundy mixed with Titanium White). Reload the brush in pale pink and add a double load of Rich Gold. Push out dabs of colour around the edge of the petals and pull the Rich Gold in to the centre of the pansy. Use the liner brush to add fine, straight lines of Burgundy coming out from the centre of the petals.

STEP THREE

Paint in the bottom petal in two coats of dark pink (Burgundy plus a touch of Titanium White). Reload the brush in dark pink, then double-load it in Rich Gold. Push out dabs of Rich Gold all around the bottom petal and pull in towards the centre. You will have to do this in three sections as the gold dabs will dry before you have a chance to pull them in, if you go all the way around the petal in one go. Make sure you keep the shape of the bottom petal correct. Use the liner brush to paint fine, straight lines of Burgundy on the bottom petal, coming out from the centre of the pansy. Make these longest in the middle and shorter on each side. Add some tiny pale pink lines to the centre of the flower and, lastly, add a dot of Titanium White roughly mixed with Yellow Oxide.

YELLOW PANSIES

Follow the method for the yellow and pink pansies but base paint all the petals in pale yellow (Titanium White with a touch of Yellow Oxide). Use Burgundy for the liner work on the side and bottom petals, then add tiny lines of Burgundy mixed equally with Diox Purple for painting the centre of the bottom petal.

PURPLE PANSIES

Base paint the top petals in pale pink (Titanium White mixed with Burgundy). The side petals are based in Burgundy mixed with Diox Purple and Titanium White (1:1:1) and the bottom petal is a darker version of the side petals, made with less Titanium White. The liner work is in Diox Purple with tiny lines of pale Diox Purple in the centre of the bottom petal.

DAB DAISIES

Load the tip of the round brush in Opal, then dip it in some Titanium White. Paint three dabs to form the top three petals of the dab daisies, then reload in Opal only for the bottom two petals. Add a centre of Burgundy roughly mixed with Titanium White to each daisy.

Detail of the powder bowl pansies and lacework

FINISHING

STEP ONE

With the cloth, wipe some antiquing patina all over the bowl, then add a tiny amount of Burnt Umber oil paint to the cloth. Rub this over the outside of the bowl and lid to give a gentle tint of colour. Intensify the antiquing inside the lid and the bowl by adding more oil paint to the cloth and wiping it onto the gold sponging. Use a bristle brush to push some undiluted oil paint into the inside corners of the bowl and blend this out with the cloth.

STEP TWO

When all the paint is completely dry, varnish the bowl and lid with five coats of gloss varnish.

FRENCH FLORAL BOX

This is a very pretty and easy project to paint. Although the preparation takes a bit of time, the actual painting is very quick. The flowers and leaves are painted using transparent washes of colour, rather than solid paint, which gives a dainty, light look to the box.

MATERIALS

Triangular pine box, 24 cm ($9^1/_2$ in) across and 8.5 cm ($3^1/_2$ in) deep
Jo Sonja's Artists Colors: Pine Green, Teal Green, French Blue, Burgundy, Indian Red Oxide, Red Earth, Yellow Oxide, Titanium White, Brown Earth
Round brush, size 3
Liner brush
1" bristle brush for base painting
Toothbrush
Black graphite paper
Fine stylus
Jo Sonja's Decor Crackle
Antiquing patina
Oil paint: Raw Sienna, Burnt Umber
Oil-based varnish, satin
Sandpaper, 320 grade
Tack cloth
Cloth

Detail of the roses on the box

PREPARATION

See the painting design on the Pull Out Pattern Sheet and the worksheet on page 49.

STEP ONE

Base paint the box with one coat of Titanium White, then sand it well. Wipe it with the tack cloth.

STEP TWO

Put out some French Blue, Pine Green and Red Earth on your palette. Add enough Titanium White to make a pastel version of each colour. Paint random-shaped and random-sized patches of each colour all over the lid and the sides of the box. Paint these patches smoothly (without texture) and make them overlap so that none of the original Titanium White is showing. I painted all the green patches first, then the blue, then the pale Red Earth so that I didn't have to keep washing out the brush between colour changes. Sand lightly.

STEP THREE

Apply varying-sized patches of the Decor Crackle here and there. When this is almost dry but still a little tacky, paint on a coat of Titanium White roughly mixed with a little Yellow Oxide. Do not overmix the white and the yellow on the palette; brush on both colours together and let the base painting brush do the mixing. This gives a slightly streaky, old look to the finished box. Be very generous when applying this colour, as you only put on one coat. Try not to go back over areas that have started to crack. Allow the paint to dry overnight.

STEP FOUR

Transfer the pattern very carefully, using the graphite paper and the fine stylus. As this project uses washes not solid colours, any stray tracing lines will show through.

Hint: When you are painting wash flowers and leaves, work quickly and use as few strokes as possible to fill out the shape required, so that you don't get overlap lines down the shapes. Make sure you roll excess paint off your brush before you start to paint, to avoid getting puddles at the end of your strokes.

PAINTING

LEAVES

STEP ONE

Wash in the leaves in a mix of Pine Green and Teal Green (1:1) with a little water added to it. Add enough water to make the colour transparent, but keep in mind you don't want it too pale or your painting will disappear altogether when you antique it.

STEP TWO

Darken the base of the leaves with a less transparent green mix (same colour, but less water). Quickly clean your brush and use it to wipe out the

edge of the shading so it fades into the original colour (see the rose leaves on the worksheet).

STEP THREE

Use the liner brush loaded in the Pine Green/Teal Green mix to outline the leaves and add a centre vein.

BLUE FLOWERS

STEP ONE

Wash these in watery French Blue. Add a stronger patch of French Blue (less water in the wash) to the centre of the flowers that are open. Wash some of the stronger French Blue onto the back petals of the flowers in profile. Outline the flowers in French Blue using the liner brush, then add some fine lines coming out on each petal from the centre of the open flowers.

STEP TWO

Paint a Titanium White centre on the open flowers. When this is dry, wash some Yellow Oxide onto one side of these centres. Add a wash of the Pine Green/Teal Green mix to the calyx of the flowers in profile and outline this in stronger Pine Green/ Teal Green mix. The stems of these flowers are also painted in the stronger green mix.

Detail of the side of the box

ROSES

Note: In each bunch of roses on the top of the box, one is painted in Burgundy, one is Indian Red Oxide and one is a mix of Burgundy and Red Earth. The following instructions apply for all the roses – just change the colour.

Wash the whole shape of the rose in Burgundy. Add a patch of stronger Burgundy to the opening at the top of the rose. Paint a C stroke of the stronger Burgundy on the outer petals, under the bowl of the rose. Paint a wash of the stronger Burgundy over the front petal on the bowl of the rose. Before this dries, clean your brush and use it to blot up some colour from the centre of this petal, leaving it lighter in the middle. Add the outlines.

BUDS

Wash the buds in Burgundy. When this is dry, outline the buds in Burgundy. Add a tiny dot of the Pine Green/Teal Green mix to the base of the bud and paint the stems in the same colour.

RIBBON

Wash in the ribbon in Yellow Oxide and outline it in stronger Yellow Oxide when the wash is dry.

SIDE OF THE LID

STEP ONE

Measure and mark off 2.5 cm (1 in) intervals around the side of the lid. Work around the marks painting a watery patch for each flower – some Burgundy, some French Blue and some Yellow Oxide. Using the corresponding colour, outline each patch by painting a loose daisy shape over the top of the patch and adding a tiny circle for a centre. Connect the daisies with a Pine Green/Teal Green stem line, then add watery comma leaves (placing two on each side of the stem). Strengthen the Pine Green/ Teal Green mix and add some extra S-stroke and comma leaves over the wash leaves already painted.

STEP TWO

Paint a fine, slightly watery line of Burgundy mixed with Red Earth (1:1) about 2 mm ($^1/_{16}$ in) above the lower edge of the lid side. Do the best you can, but don't worry if it's a little wavy or uneven as this will only complement the style of the box. Add a tiny scallop edge above this line all the way around. Paint this same line and scallop edge around the top edge of the lid side, close to the edge.

GARLAND

Paint comma leaves and S-stroke leaves in a watery Pine Green/Teal Green mix along both sides of the garland. When this is dry, add extra leaves, overlapping the wash ones, in a stronger Pine Green/Teal Green mix. Add the ribbon, roses (in Burgundy), rose leaves and daisies as per the directions for those on top of the box.

FINISHING

STEP ONE

Paint the inside of the box in Titanium White roughly mixed with a little French Blue, allowing the brush to do most of the mixing for you.

STEP TWO

Using the toothbrush, speckle the outside of the box with Brown Earth. Antique by rubbing a cloth with some antiquing patina all over the box. Add a smudge of Raw Sienna oil paint to the cloth and wipe this over the box. Darken the edges of the lid and the sides of the box by brushing on some undiluted Burnt Umber oil paint and blending this out with the cloth.

Hint: Using Raw Sienna to antique pale-coloured projects gives a lovely warm glow and is an interesting alternative to Burnt Umber.

STEP THREE

Varnish with three coats of varnish.

HUMMINGBIRD SECRETAIRE

I have used gold-edged pansies and fuchsias twisting around a golden cord as a backdrop for the hummingbird on this secretaire. The gilding on the edges of the box enhances the overall richness of this project which is one of my favourite pieces.

It is very important that this piece be painted using brushes which are in excellent condition. This secretaire is one of the most difficult projects in the book, but with a little patience and delicate brush work I'm sure you will be happy with your results.

MATERIALS

- MDF secretaire measuring 36 cm x 25 cm (14¼ in x 10 in)
- Jo Sonja's Artists Colors: Titanium White, Pine Green, Teal Green, Yellow Oxide, Diox Purple, Burgundy, Raw Sienna, Burnt Sienna, Ultramarine, Jade, Rich Gold, Opal, Carbon Black
- Round brush, size 3
- Liner brush
- 1" bristle brush
- Plastic kitchen wrap
- Jo Sonja's Tannin Blocking Sealer
- Imitation gold leaf
- Cotton gloves
- Steel wool, 0000 grade
- Antiquing patina
- Stylus
- Sandpaper
- Tack cloth
- Oil paint, Burnt Umber
- White graphite paper
- Oil-based varnish, gloss

PREPARATION

See the painting designs on the Pull Out Pattern Sheet and the worksheet on page 55.

STEP ONE

Remove the hinges and the dividers from the inside of the box. Base paint the inside of the box, the inside of the drawer and the dividers with two or three coats of Jade, sanding well between coats. Be careful not to allow thick paint to pool in the slots where the dividers fit or you may not be able to slide the dividers back in!

STEP TWO

Base paint the outside of the secretaire in a 1:1 mix of Pine Green and Teal Green. Apply two or three coats, sanding between each coat.

STEP THREE

Mix some Jade into the 1:1 mix of Pine Green and Teal Green, then dilute it with water. Test the colour on a sample board, before painting, to determine how watery you want the Jade/Pine Green/Teal Green mix to be. Marble the outside of the box, using the plastic kitchen wrap and following the instructions on page 6.

STEP FOUR

Trace the pattern and transfer it to the secretaire, using the white graphite paper and stylus.

PAINTING

CORD AND TASSELS

STEP ONE

Paint a watery coat of Yellow Oxide over the tassels and the cord using the round brush. When this is dry, load the brush in slightly runny Raw Sienna, then double-load it in Rich Gold. Paint comma strokes lying close together to give the impression of the twists in the cord.

STEP TWO

Paint the knot of the tassels in two coats of Rich Gold then, using the liner brush, add the fringes in the same colour. Add some shading to the tassels by painting a little Burnt Sienna above and below the knot with the round brush, blending out the shading with a clean, damp brush, before the edge of the Burnt Sienna has a chance to dry.

STEP THREE

Outline the centre of the knot, using the liner brush loaded in Burnt Sienna. Add some lines of Burnt Sienna on the fringe of the tassels, then crosshatch the centre of the knot on the tassels with Burnt Sienna.

PANSY LEAVES

STEP ONE

Base the leaves in Pine Green, using the round brush.

STEP TWO

Reload the brush in Pine Green and add a double load of Rich Gold to one side of the brush. Work one side of the leaf at a time, keeping the Rich Gold side of the brush facing towards the outer side of the leaf. Push out dabs of Rich Gold down the side of the leaf. Quickly touch the tip of the brush into the gold dabs and pull them in towards the centre of the leaf. Keep these pulling strokes at an angle that will help give the impression of the veins of the leaf. Do the same for the other side of the leaf, then add a centre vein in Rich Gold using the liner brush.

PANSIES

Refer to the instructions and step-by-step work sheet for painting the pansies on page 42. The colours used are:

• Pansy 1: Top petals in Titanium White with a touch of Yellow Oxide; side petals in pale pink (Titanium White with a touch of Burgundy) with Burgundy liner work; and the bottom petal in dark pink (Burgundy with a touch of Titanium White) with Burgundy liner work, then pale pink liner work on the top.

• Pansy 2: Top petals in pale purple (Titanium White with a touch of Diox Purple); side petals in medium purple (Titanium White with a little more Diox Purple) with Diox Purple liner work; and the bottom petal in dark purple (Diox Purple with touch of Titanium White) with Diox Purple liner work, then medium purple liner work on top.

• Pansy 3: Top petals in pale yellow (Titanium White with a touch of Yellow Oxide); side petals in medium yellow (Titanium White with a little more Yellow Oxide) with Burgundy liner work; and the bottom petal in the same colours as the side petals with Burgundy liner work, then pale pink liner work on top.

• Pansy 4: Top petals in pale pink (Titanium White, with a touch of Burgundy); side petals in medium pink (Titanium White with a little more Burgundy) with Burgundy liner work; and the bottom petal in dark pink (Burgundy with a touch of Titanium White) with Burgundy liner work, then pale pink liner work on top.

• Pansy buds: Side petals in pale purple (Titanium White with a touch of Diox Purple); and the centre petal in dark purple (Diox Purple with a touch of Titanium White).

All the pansies have a centre dot of pale yellow (Yellow Oxide mixed with Titanium White).

FUCHSIA LEAVES

Base paint these leaves in Pine Green, using the round brush. When the paint is dry, reload the brush in Pine Green, then dip the tip of the brush into some Rich Gold. Place comma strokes along the leaf, coming out from the centre vein on either side. Work from the base of the leaf down towards the tip. Add a centre vein in Pine Green mixed with Rich Gold, using the liner brush.

FUCHSIAS

STEP ONE

Base paint the purple petals of the fuchsias in Diox Purple, mixed with a touch of Titanium White. When the paint is dry, reload in the same colour and add a double load of Rich Gold to the brush. Keeping the gold facing the lower edge of the flower, paint little dabs along the edge, then use the tip of the brush to pull up the gold towards the centre of the flower.

STEP TWO

Base paint the pink calyx and petals of the fuchsia in Burgundy. When the paint is dry, add a Rich Gold edge to each petal and calyx by painting a brush stroke of Burgundy double-loaded in Rich Gold along the base-painted shapes.

STEP THREE

Paint the stems, using the liner brush loaded in Pine Green mixed with a little Rich Gold. Add a Pine Green dot double-loaded in Rich Gold to the top of each fuchsia where the stem joins the flower. Use the liner brush to add three or four gold straight comma strokes to the bottom of each open flower.

WHITE FLOWERS AND BUDS

STEP ONE

Paint in the shape of these flowers and buds with two or three coats of Opal. Load the round brush in Opal, double-loaded in Titanium White and place tiny dabs around the edges of each petal, keeping the brush angled so that the white faces the outside of the petal. Work one petal at a time. Quickly pull the white in towards the centre of the flower with tiny strokes, using the tip of the brush.

STEP TWO

Using the round brush, stipple some Titanium White in the centre of the flowers. While this is still wet, add a touch of Burgundy to the same brush and stipple this onto one side of the white centre.

STEP THREE

Paint the buds with a small stroke of Opal, double-loaded in Titanium White, coming down one side, from the tip towards the stem.

STEP FOUR

Paint the stems in Pine Green double-loaded in Jade, then add a dot of Jade double-loaded in Titanium White to join the buds to their stems.

FORGET-ME-NOTS

STEP ONE

These forget-me-nots are painted with five petals – three light and two dark. Use varying shades of Diox Purple roughly mixed with Ultramarine and tiny amounts of Titanium White for the dark petals. Touch the tip of the brush into extra Titanium White for the light petals, while it is still loaded in the Diox Purple/Ultramarine mix. Don't overblend the white, but rather let the brush blend the colours on your painting. This will produce a variety of striped petals.

STEP TWO

Add a tiny dot of Yellow Oxide double-loaded in Titanium White for the centre of each flower, keeping the Titanium White facing towards the lighter petals.

HUMMINGBIRD

STEP ONE

Mix a violet colour out of Diox Purple, Ultramarine and Titanium White (equal parts of each). Base paint the bird's body in this colour, then double-load the same colour on the round brush with a darker violet (Diox Purple, Ultramarine and only a touch of Titanium White). Use this to paint the tail feathers using fine comma strokes.

STEP TWO

Base paint the bird's tummy in Opal, bringing wispy little strokes of Opal over the top edge of the tail feathers. The back wing is based in dark violet and the front wing is based in Opal. Highlight the outer edge of the tummy by painting a stroke of Opal, double-loaded in Titanium White down the edge, keeping the white towards the outer side. Add a touch of pink (Burgundy mixed with Titanium White) to the upper edge of the tummy in the same way.

STEP THREE

Highlight the bird's head, painting a stroke of violet, double-loaded in a paler violet, around the top of the head. Flick tiny strokes of violet from the body onto the pink shading on the bird's tummy.

STEP FOUR

Highlight the back wing by lightening the top edge of the wing with violet and working it down towards the lower edge. Add a violet edge to the top of the front wing, then use the liner brush to paint a Diox Purple line under this edge and a pale violet line along the top of the edge.

STEP FIVE

Load the liner brush in violet, then double-load it in pale violet. Use this to paint thin straight comma strokes from the outer edge of each wing in towards the body.

STEP SIX

Block the eye in Carbon Black, then add a small grey (Carbon Black mixed with a touch of Titanium White) comma highlight on the right side of the eye. Outline the right side only of the eye in grey, then paint fine lines coming out from this outline.

FILLER FLOWERS AND LEAVES

STEP ONE

Paint the stems in Jade with the liner brush, then add tiny buds of Yellow Oxide, double-loaded in Titanium White on the inner side of the curve of the stems.

STEP TWO

Load the round brush in Pine Green, then double-load it in Rich Gold. Paint fine comma stroke leaves around the stems of the filler flowers.

FINISHING

STEP ONE

Replace the hinges, then gild the edges of the lid, the side edges, the knob of the drawer and around the base of the secretaire. Refer to page 9 for gilding instructions.

STEP TWO

Antique the whole secretaire lightly by rubbing some patina on a cloth over it, inside and out. Add a small amount of oil paint to the same cloth and gently rub this over the box to give a mellow tone to the painting and the gilding. Strengthen the colour of the antiquing around the edges on the painting area of the lid by applying more oil paint with a brush, then blending out the edges of the colour with a cloth.

STEP THREE

When the secretaire is completely dry, varnish it and the dividers with three to five coats of gloss varnish, drying between coats. Take care not to build up too much varnish on the inside of the slots where the dividers will go.

Detail of the hummingbird

STILL LIFE WITH CHERRIES

This delicious-looking bowl of cherries, sitting on a checked tablecloth, has a distinctively country flavour. The rustic, distressed frame is complemented by the heavy antiquing.

MATERIALS

Pine frame and backing board, 40 cm x 36 cm (16 in x 14¼ in), the painting surface is 26 cm x 22 cm (10¼ in x 8¾ in)
Jo Sonja's Artists Colors: Paynes Gray, Warm White, Napthol Crimson, Yellow Oxide, Teal Green, Vermilion, Burgundy, Pine Green
Round brush, size 3
Liner brush
Bristle brush, size 4 or 5
Sandpaper, 320 grade
Antiquing patina
Cloth
Oil paint, Burnt Umber
Two extra bristle brushes, size 0, for antiquing
Langridge Artist Colours Crackle Varnish
Jo Sonja's Clear Glazing Medium
Oil-based varnish, satin
Black graphite paper
Stylus

PREPARATION

See the painting design on page 77 and the worksheet on page 59.

The preparation for this project is the same as for the Bowl of Pears on page 32, except that you need not trace on the cherries at this stage. Trace only the bowl and the tablecloth.

PAINTING

BACKGROUND

STEP ONE

Paint the background of the picture, above the bowl, in two or three coats of Paynes Gray. Add a 'halo' of lightened Paynes Gray roughly around the area where the cherries will be. Using the bristle brush, loaded in Paynes Gray and dipped into Warm White, paint rough, choppy strokes in different directions to lighten the background close to the cherries, gradually fading the halo off into the dark blue of the background. Increase the amount of Paynes Gray on the brush and lessen the Warm White as you work away from the cherries.

STEP TWO

Trace the cherries, leaves and stems and transfer them, using the graphite paper and stylus.

LEAVES

STEP ONE

Base paint the leaves in Teal Green. Load the round brush in Teal Green and double-load it in Napthol Crimson. Paint a casual stroke down the lower edge of each leaf, keeping the Napthol Crimson on the outer side. Roughly work this in towards the centre of the leaf, approximately one-third of the way.

STEP TWO

Reload the brush in Teal Green and add a double load of a cream colour (made with Warm White plus a touch of Yellow Oxide). Keeping the cream to the upper edge of the leaf, lighten the top edge of each leaf with a casual stroke, working the paint in towards the centre. Leave some Teal Green showing between the Napthol Crimson and the cream. Use the bristle brush to dry-brush a little cream on the lighter side of each leaf.

TABLECLOTH

STEP ONE

Add a little Warm White to some Paynes Gray and paint all the blue checks. I used the liner brush to get into the corners, then filled in the rest of the square with the round brush. When the paint is dry, dry-brush Paynes Gray in the bottom left-hand corner of each blue square (where the corner is visible) using the bristle brush. Dry-brush the blue check colour in the lower left-hand corner of all the white squares. Mix in some extra white and add some dry brushing of this light Paynes Gray on the top right corner of the blue squares and across the top of the blue squares on the folded section of the cloth to add highlights.

STEP TWO

Using the liner, paint in the detail lines on the tablecloth in Napthol Crimson.

BOWL

STEP ONE

Load the round brush in Warm White and double-load in pale Paynes Gray on one side of the brush. Stroke this down the sides of the bowl, keeping the pale blue to the outside. Work what is left of the colour on the brush in towards the centre of the bowl – about one-third of the way. Shade under the top rim of the bowl and under the lower edge onto the foot of the bowl, in the same way.

STEP TWO

Load the liner brush in watery Paynes Gray and paint small S strokes along the top rim of the bowl.

CHERRIES

STEP ONE

Paint a watery wash of Burgundy in between the cherries. Base paint all the cherries in three or four coats of Napthol Crimson. When these are dry, shade the lower left-hand side of each cherry by painting on a stroke of Napthol Crimson, double-loaded in Burgundy. Where the edge of a cherry is covered by another one, do not add any shading. Highlight the upper right side of the cherries in the same way, adding a stroke of Napthol Crimson, double-loaded in Vermilion.

STEP TWO

Using the bristle brush, dry-brush some Yellow Oxide mixed with Vermilion on the light side of the cherries. Add a touch of Warm White to the Yellow Oxide/Vermilion mix and dry-brush an extra highlight on the front cherries only.

STEMS

Add a smallish dot of Burgundy to the cherries to form a hollow where the stalk joins. Note that not all the cherries have this hollow visible (refer to the painting design). Paint all the stems in Teal Green, double-loaded in a small amount of Warm White.

FRAME

Paint the frame in the same way as the one for the pears on page 32, substituting Paynes Gray mixed with a touch of Warm White for the Pine Green/Teal Green mix.

FINISHING

Speckle the board with Brown Earth. Antique and crackle the picture using the same method as for the Bowl of Pears on page 32.

Detail of the bowl with cherries

COUNTRY-STYLE GAME BOARD

This game board is painted in the same Petrikivka style as the Ukrainian-style Lap Desk on page 14, but I have changed the colouring from the traditional primary range to colours that give a more rustic, country feel. Heavily distress and antique your project to make it look like a family heirloom that has been enjoyed for generations.

MATERIALS

MDF game board, 28 cm x 23.5 cm (11 in x 9¼ in)
Hexagonal box
Twenty-four heart-shaped counters
Jo Sonja's Artists Colors: Smoked Pearl, Yellow Oxide, Burgundy, Red Earth, Teal Green, Storm Blue, Titanium White, Brown Earth
Round brush, size 3
Liner brush
½" flat brush or something similar for painting the squares
Stylus
Scotch Magic Tape
1" bristle brush
Black graphite paper
Jo Sonja's Flow Medium
Antiquing patina
Oil paint, Burnt Umber
Oil-based varnish, satin
Sandpaper, 320 grade
Tack cloth
Cloth for antiquing

PREPARATION

See the painting design on the Pull Out Pattern Sheet and the worksheet on page 63.

STEP ONE

Base paint the board and the counter box in two or three rough coats of Smoked Pearl, sanding well between coats. Aim to have some brush strokes and texture showing in the base painting as this will help to give an aged appearance when the pieces are given an antique finish.

STEP TWO

Base paint half of the counters in two coats of Yellow Oxide and the other half in a 1:1 mix of Burgundy and Red Earth. Sand the edges of the counters to distress them.

STEP THREE

Trace the pattern and transfer it to the board and box, using the graphite paper and stylus. Do not press too hard as a faint imprint is all that is needed and dark graphite lines may show through some of the lighter coloured flowers. Using a ruler when tracing the straight lines will help to keep them straight.

PAINTING

CHEQUERBOARD

STEP ONE

Mask off alternate rows of squares on the board using long pieces of Scotch Magic Tape.

STEP TWO

Paint in the blue squares using the flat brush, loaded in a 1:1 mix of Storm Blue and Titanium White. When the blue paint is dry, peel off the tape and mask off the other rows of squares and paint the blue checks in the same pale blue mix.

STEP THREE

Divide each panel of the counter box into checks, mask them off and paint the squares in a pale Storm Blue.

FLOWERS AND LEAVES

Hint: Add two or three drops of flow medium to each colour of paint before you start your stroke-work flowers and leaves. The flow medium will help to make your strokes glide on without making them transparent.

STEP ONE

Mix up three shades of Teal Green by adding a touch of Teal Green to some Titanium White for the palest shade, by mixing Teal Green and Titanium White in equal parts for the medium shade, and by using Teal Green on its own for the darkest shade.

STEP TWO

Load the round brush in the medium shade, then double-load it in the palest one. Paint comma strokes down one side of each leaf, starting from the tip of the leaf and keeping the pale shade to the outer side of the brush. Make sure you keep your strokes close to each other so that none of the background shows through. Reload your brush as you need to.

STEP THREE

Load the brush in the medium teal and add a double load of Teal Green to one side of the brush. Paint comma strokes down the other side of the leaf, starting at the tip, keeping the Teal Green to

the outer side of the brush. Paint all the comma leaves, using the medium teal double loaded in Teal Green.

STEP FOUR

The stem lines are all painted in a watery medium teal, using the liner brush.

FLOWERS

• Flower 1: Paint the main petals, using the round brush loaded in Red Earth with a double load of Burgundy. Keep the Burgundy towards the top edge of each petal. Some petals may need two strokes to fill out their shape. Load the brush in Yellow Oxide and dip the tip into some Titanium White. Paint tiny straight comma strokes to form the hearts at the top of the flower. Paint a Teal Green stem line from each heart into the centre of the flower and add a Red Earth calyx to the base of the hearts. The centre of the flower is Titanium White.

• Flower 2: The main petals of this flower are the same as Flower 1. Use four strokes for the centre petal, keeping the Burgundy to the outside of the petal (one stroke on each side and two strokes to make up the centre). Paint small comma strokes of Yellow Oxide, double-loaded in Titanium White for the centre of the flower. Use the stylus to add Titanium White dots around the lower edge of the yellow centre. Start in the middle and work out on one side first, then reload the stylus and do the other side so that the largest dots are in the centre of the flower and they become smaller as they go towards the outer edge. Use the liner brush to paint long, thin straight comma strokes at the top of the flower.

• Flower 3: Start with the main petals, using Red Earth double-loaded in Burgundy (refer to Flower 2). Load the brush in Yellow Oxide, double-loaded in Titanium White. Keeping the Titanium White to the outside, paint the two long comma strokes around the centre. Use two strokes to paint the middle section of the centre, keeping the Titanium White to the outer edge on both strokes. Add tiny dots under the yellow centre using the stylus, with the largest in the middle and reducing in size towards the outside. Add three Burgundy dots on each side and then use the liner brush to paint long Titanium White comma strokes on the sides of the flower.

Detail of the game board

WHITE BERRIES

Paint the berries with two or three coats of Titanium White. Add tiny strokes of Teal Green off the end of each berry. Paint Teal Green stems using the liner brush.

ORANGE BERRIES

Mix some Red Earth and Yellow Oxide together to make orange. Use this mix to paint in the berries. Use the liner brush to add a small Titanium White comma stroke on the left side of each berry. Paint the stems with Teal Green.

BUDS

Load the brush in Yellow Oxide and add a double-load of Red Earth. Paint three strokes to form the bud. Use the liner brush to add tiny Teal Green sepals coming from the stem up onto the bud. Paint the stems with Teal Green.

FINISHING

STEP ONE

Mask off the line between the checks and the floral design, using the Scotch Magic Tape. Paint this line in one coat of Burgundy, roughly mixed with Red Earth. Don't worry if this is a little uneven or transparent.

STEP TWO

Measure in 1 cm ($^3/_8$ in) all around the edge of the board and paint this in the same way as the line in step 1. You will be able to mask off the straight edges, but you will have to paint the rounded ends freehand.

STEP THREE

Paint the edges, the back of the board and the top and bottom rims of the counter box in the Burgundy/Red Earth mix.

STEP FOUR

Distress the board and the box by sanding the painting, especially the checks. Wipe with the tack cloth. Using the toothbrush, speckle with Brown Earth.

STEP FIVE

Antique all the counters, the board and the box by rubbing them with the cloth dipped in antiquing patina. Add a small amount of Burnt Umber oil paint to the cloth and wipe this all over the pieces. Darken the antiquing around the edge of the board by applying more oil paint with the bristle brush, then blending the paint out with the cloth. Intensify the antiquing around the lower edge and inside the counter box.

STEP SIX

When all the paint is dry, varnish with three coats of satin oil-based varnish.

TEDDY BEAR PHOTO ALBUM

What can I say about teddies except that I love them! I especially like old, worn and cherished bears. This small photo album would make a great gift for a new baby or for a bear lover of any age.

MATERIALS

Small pine photo album,
22 cm x 19 cm ($8^3/_4$ in x $7^1/_2$ in)
Jo Sonja's Artists Colors: Warm White, French Blue, Raw Sienna, Burnt Sienna, Yellow Oxide, Carbon Black, Burgundy, Red Earth, Brown Earth
Round brush, size 3
Liner brush
Flat brush, size 8
1" bristle brush for base painting
Toothbrush
Scotch Magic Tape
Chalk pencil
Sandpaper, 320 grade
Black graphite paper
Stylus
Paper
Ruler
Antiquing patina
Cloth
Oil paint, Burnt Umber
Oil-based varnish, satin

PREPARATION

See the painting design on page 79 and the worksheet on page 67.

STEP ONE

Remove the hinges and base paint the front cover with three or four coats of Warm White. Use rough, choppy strokes to build up texture and sand lightly between each coat. Base paint the back cover, front spine and the inside of both the back and front covers with two or three coats of French Blue.

STEP TWO

Trace the design and transfer it to the album cover, using the graphite paper and stylus.

PAINTING

BACKGROUND

STEP ONE

Use Scotch Magic Tape to mask off a 1 cm ($^3/_8$ in) border around the top, right side and bottom edge of the front cover. Paint this area with one coat of French Blue.

STEP TWO

Mark off 1 cm ($^3/_8$ in) stripes using the chalk pencil and ruler. Paint these casually, using the round brush loaded in watery French Blue mixed with a little Warm White. Do not worry if these lines are a little wavering as this will add to the overall effect of the picture. Paint tiny fine dashes of watery French Blue with the liner brush down each side of each stripe. If you prefer a more precise look, mask off the stripes with Scotch Magic Tape and paint them with a thicker mixture of French Blue and Warm White. Distress the blue border and stripes by sanding them lightly.

Hint: Watery paint will bleed under the edges of the tape so use undiluted paint to avoid this problem.

STEP THREE

Using the round brush, paint the area under the bear. Load the brush with French Blue and paint the top edge quickly. Load Warm White onto the same brush and work this paler French Blue down the area using quick horizontal strokes. Gradually fade off this colour as it comes closer to the bottom edge by adding more and more Warm White.

TEDDY

Note: My teddies are painted in three stages. The first stage involves using the round brush to dab in the three shades of colour used (dark, medium and light). The second stage blends the shading between the colours as you apply a second coat and the last stage is the adding of individual hairs with a liner brush.

STEP ONE

Paint the areas on your bear marked L (for light) on the pattern in a cream colour (Warm White mixed with a touch of Yellow Oxide). Use short dabbing strokes following the direction of the pile of the fur. Do not add too much texture with your dabs as it will then be difficult to paint the fur later. Add Raw Sienna to the brush and dab in the areas marked M (for medium). Use Burnt Sienna to dab in the areas marked D (dark).

STEP TWO

Add a second coat of each colour, but this time blend the edges between the shades more, so that there are no hard

C
1
B

edges of colour, but rather a gentle transition from light to dark. Base paint the teddy's paw pads in cream, then add a dash of Warm White to the same brush and roughly paint a highlight in the centre of each pad. Add the split in the left leg in Burgundy, then use the liner brush to paint the loose thread in Warm White.

STEP THREE

Base paint teddy's coat in French Blue mixed with a little Warm White. Paint the collar in Warm White. Shade the jacket by painting some slightly watery French Blue under the collar and down the sides of the chest. Before this dries, clean the brush, then use it to blend out the outer edge of the shading. If you prefer you could float the shading on instead with a flat brush (see page 8). Highlight the left-hand edge of the sleeves in the same way, using a slightly watery pale French Blue. Add a stripe of French Blue around the collar and two stripes of pale French Blue around the edges of the sleeves.

STEP FOUR

Base paint the sails of the boat in Warm White, then brush a little Yellow Oxide onto the centre of each sail. Paint the hull of the boat and the flag in a 1:1 mix of Burgundy and Red Earth. Add a touch of Warm White to the Burgundy/ Red Earth mix and roughly highlight the top edge of the boat and the flag. The mast and the yardarm are painted in Burnt Sienna with the liner brush.

STEP FIVE

Using the liner brush, paint fine hairs all over the bear, following the direction of the pile. Use Burnt Sienna for the dark fur around the lower edges of the legs, face and right sides of the arms. Add Raw Sienna fur all over the bear and cream fur on the top of the ears and head, left sides of the arms and top of the legs.

EYES

Referring to the worksheet, base paint the eyes in Yellow Oxide. Add a Burnt Sienna iris. When this is dry, paint a small circle in Carbon Black in the centre of the iris for the pupil. Add a tiny comma highlight on the lower left side of the iris in a mix of Burnt Sienna and Yellow Oxide. Paint a tiny Warm White dot on the top right side of the iris. Outline the whole eye in Carbon Black. I leave this outlining until the eye is completely dry, as I often have to correct the black by wiping it off with a damp cotton bud and this will not disturb the rest of the eye if it is dry.

NOSE

Using the round brush, paint the nose in Burnt Sienna, then highlight it by painting on a few vertical dashes with Warm White added to the brush. Paint some tiny stitches coming down from the nose to the mouth in Burnt Sienna.

FINISHING

Speckle the front cover with Brown Earth. Reassemble the covers, then antique the whole album lightly by rubbing the cloth dampened with antiquing patina all over it. Add a tiny smudge of Burnt Umber oil paint to the same cloth and wipe it over the covers to give a gentle, mellow tone. Be careful not to make the teddy bear too dark. Intensify the antiquing around the edge of the front cover and around the hinges by applying more oil paint with a bristle brush, then blending the paint out with the cloth. When the album cover is thoroughly dry, varnish it with three coats of varnish. Reassemble the album.

Detail of teddy bear photo album

UTENSIL HOLDER

I have painted this design on a small, half-round utensil holder, but it would adapt well to many other articles. It is a smaller version of the Fruit Platter on page 10.

MATERIALS

- Pine utensil holder, 24 cm x 14 cm ($9\frac{1}{2}$ in x $5\frac{1}{2}$ in)
- Jo Sonja's Artists Colors: Titanium White, Rich Gold, Carbon Black, Yellow Oxide, Yellow Light, Diox Purple, Storm Blue, Burgundy, Antique Green, Burnt Sienna, Raw Sienna, Napthol Crimson
- Round brush, size 3
- Liner brush
- Bristle brush, size 5
- Toothbrush
- Antiquing patina
- Cloth
- Oil paint, Burnt Umber
- Two extra bristle brushes, size 0 (for antiquing)
- Scotch Magic Tape
- White graphite paper
- Stylus
- Sandpaper, 320 grade
- Oil-based varnish, gloss

PREPARATION

See the painting design on page 78 and the worksheet on page 71.

STEP ONE

Base coat the utensil holder with two or three coats of Rich Gold, sanding well between coats.

STEP TWO

Transfer the design using the white graphite paper and stylus.

Hint: I have used a round brush to base and shade all the fruit; you could use a flat brush if you prefer.

PAINTING

APPLES

Base paint the apples in three or four coats of Napthol Crimson. Using the bristle brush, dry-brush some Yellow Oxide onto the right shoulder of the apples. Use slightly curving strokes and avoid the hollow on the apple where the stalk will go. Add some Yellow Light to the brush and intensify this highlight by adding more dry brushing in the centre of the Yellow Oxide.

PEAR

STEP ONE

Base paint the pear in Yellow Oxide, then load the round brush in Yellow Oxide with a double loading of Raw Sienna. Paint a stroke down the dark side of the pear, with the Raw Sienna towards the outside of the stroke. Work this shading in casually towards the centre of the pear.

STEP TWO

Reload the brush in Yellow Oxide and add a double load of cream (Titanium White with a touch of Yellow Oxide). Stroke this down the light side of the pear, working it into the middle. Dry-brush Raw Sienna over the dark side, cream on the light side and, finally, Yellow Oxide in the centre to blend the shading together. Dry-brush a tiny touch of Napthol Crimson on the bottom of the dark side of the pear.

PEACHES

Base paint the peaches in a mix of Yellow Oxide, Yellow Light and Titanium White (1:1:1). Mix a touch of Napthol Crimson into some Yellow Light to make orange. Load the round brush in the peach base colour and double-load it with orange. Paint a stroke around the outside of the peach, roughly blending the colour in and keeping the orange to the outside of the peach. Reload the brush in the same colours and paint this around the top edge of the centre section of the peach. Dry-brush orange on top of the shading to soften the blending. Add some dry brushing of cream to the centre of the front section of the peach.

PURPLE PLUMS

Mix some Diox Purple with some Burgundy (1:1), then add a touch of Titanium White. Base paint the plums in this mix. Lighten the base colour with some extra Titanium White and highlight the top edge of the plum and the top edge of the front section of the plum by loading the brush in the plum colour, then adding a double load of the paler plum colour. Soften the highlighting by dry-brushing some of the paler plum colour over the blending.

BLUE GRAPES

Base paint the grapes in Diox Purple mixed with Storm Blue (1:1) with a touch of Titanium White added. Follow the outline of each bunch of grapes, then just fill in all the centre of the bunch. Trace the shape of the grapes back on. Highlight the top right of each grape by painting a stroke of the base colour, double-loaded in the paler

version (add a little Titanium White) around the edge of each grape, keeping the pale colour to the outside of each grape. Add some extra Titanium White to the paler base colour and dry-brush this on the grapes.

LEAVES

STEP ONE

Base paint the leaves in Antique Green. Load the brush in Antique Green, then double-load in Napthol Crimson. Paint a casual stroke along the lower edge of each leaf, keeping the Napthol Crimson to the outer edge of the leaf. Work this roughly in towards the centre of the leaf (about one-third of the way).

STEP TWO

Reload in Antique Green, then double-load in cream. Paint a stroke along the top edge of each leaf, keeping the cream to the outer edge. Work this in towards the middle of the leaf (about one-third of the way). Dry-brush some of the cream onto the light side of the leaves to roughly soften the shading, using the bristle brush.

STALKS

Using the liner brush, paint the stalks in Burnt Sienna lightened with a touch of Titanium White.

FINISHING

STEP ONE

Speckle the utensil holder with Burnt Sienna. Using the tape, mask off a straight border, about 2–3 mm (1/16 in) wide around the top and the bottom. Paint in Carbon Black.

STEP TWO

Paint the side edges of the back of the utensil holder in Carbon Black. Antique the utensil holder by placing some patina on a cloth and rubbing it all over the article. Add a smudge of Burnt Umber oil paint to the same cloth and wipe this over the utensil holder to give it an even tint of colour.

STEP THREE

Use the oil paint to build up shadows between the pieces of fruit by applying undiluted paint with one of the small bristle brushes. Blend out the edge of the shading with the other small bristle brush, wherever one piece of fruit overlaps another. The shadow should fall on the fruit at the back.

Hint: Shading the grapes takes some time and it is difficult to stop some of the antiquing shadows getting onto the grapes in front of the shading. I use a cotton bud dipped in a little antiquing patina to clean up the edges when I have finished the shading.

STEP FOUR

Intensify the antiquing around the edge of the utensil holder by applying more oil paint with the bristle brush, then blending the paint out with the cloth. See the picture for a guide.

STEP FIVE

When the paint is completely dry, varnish the outside of the utensil holder with four or five coats of varnish.

Detail of the utensil holder

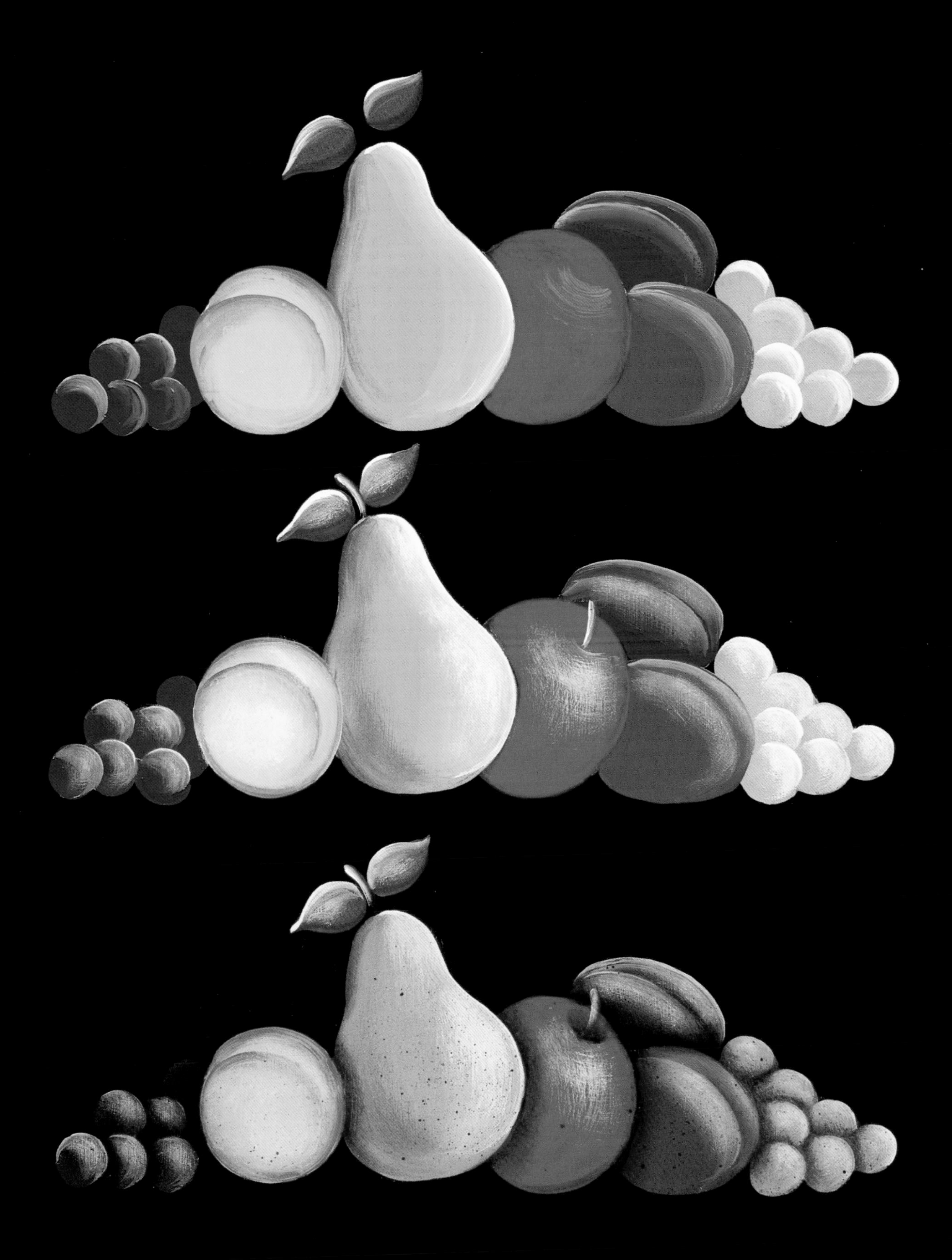

CHEDDAR.

PARTRIDGE PLATE

Follow the painting design below for Partridge Plate on page 28.
Photocopy pattern at 100%.

ZHOSTOVA CHOCOLATE BOX

Follow the painting design below for Zhostova Chocolate Box on page 19.
Photocopy pattern at 100%.

GOLD LACE AND PANSY BOWL

Follow the painting design below for Gold Lace and Pansy Bowl on page 42.
Photocopy pattern at 100%.

NAIVE STILL LIFE – BOWL OF PEARS

Follow the painting design below for Naive Still Life – Bowl of Pears on page 32.
Shown here at 75% of size. Enlarge pattern on the photocopier at 125%.

STILL LIFE WITH CHERRIES

Follow the painting design below for Still Life with Cherries on page 56.
Shown here at 75% of size. Enlarge pattern on the photocopier at 125%.

UTENSIL HOLDER

Follow the painting design below for Utensil Holder on page 68.
Photocopy pattern at 100%.

TEDDY BEAR PHOTO ALBUM

Follow the painting design below for Teddy Bear Photo Album on page 64.
Photocopy pattern at 100%.

ACKNOWLEDGMENTS

There have been many people who have helped and encouraged me in putting this book together. I would especially like to thank my husband, Peter, for his complete confidence in me – 'Of course you can write a book', he said.

Thanks also to my children, Catherine and Samantha for their patience; my parents, for their unending support of whatever I do; Sue Schirmer, the instigator of this project (another 'kitchen table' production); Heleen Van Der Haar, who taught me to paint; and Enid Hoessinger, who encouraged me to keep painting.

Finally, thanks to all my students for their friendship and laughter.

Sue

All the wood pieces (except for the chocolate box) used for the projects in this book were generously supplied by the Victorian Academy of Decorative Art, 369 Camberwell Road, Camberwell Victoria 3124, (03) 9882 7082.

The chocolate box was supplied by Romantique, 68 Milton Parade, Malvern Victoria 3144, (03) 9822 5293.